Trees
in a Winter
Landscape

Trees
in a Winter
Landscape
by
Alice
Upham
Smith

Holt, Rinehart and Winston
New York   Chicago   San Francisco

Published simultaneously in Canada by Holt, Rinehart and Winston of Canada, Limited.

Library of Congress Catalog Card Number: 77-80347

First Edition

Designer: Todd Ash

SBN: 03-081863-x

Printed in the United States of America

In loving memory of my father,
Thomas Francis Upham,
Who taught me to appreciate trees

Contents

A tree, depending on its shape, can be a canopy of shade, a shadow tracery against a wall, a column or space divider, or an ornament that is a focus for a garden design. Some trees are for little boys to climb and some provide sturdy branches for hanging a swing.

Most of us know what trees look like during the growing season. In the spring, we watch the swelling buds and opening blossoms. In summer, we prize the cooling shade of the green branches, and in fall, we admire the bright color of the leaves. But in winter, the trees seem finished, the show is done. Yet it is in winter that the artful symmetry of the trees can be seen, when the structure stands out stark and bare against the sky.

An artist learning to draw is often taught to study the human form to learn proportion. A tree is also a good model in proportion, with a strong sturdy trunk subdividing into large branches, smaller branches, and finally all twigs, in perfect symmetry. Each species has a completely different habit of growth, a special way of making these divisions so that one can easily tell one kind of tree from another by the silhouette and branching patterns. There are, of course, other clues to winter identification, such as bark, twigs, buds, and seedpods, and they are included in this book for reference. Professor Charles Sprague Sargent's classic *Manual of the Trees of North America* has been a reference for many of the technical names provided in this book, and, in some additional cases, names appearing in recent tree books have been used.

It is the appearance of the tree as a whole and its essential character, however, that is important in the landscape. With more and more picture windows, interest is focused on the outdoor scene, especially during the long winter months when the flowers are gone.

Differences in the character of trees can add not only beauty but distinction to the landscape. See how rugged and gnarled a Red Oak is, how well it looks with rough masonry. On the other hand, a Beech, though majestic and massive, is fine and elegant; a Birch is dainty. The drawings in this book show the easily recognizable winter features of some of our best-loved and common trees, naturalized as well as native, decorative as well as forest trees. Drawings have been used to show the trees without any distracting scenery and to emphasize the individuality of the various species.

Plants are the elements out of which we build landscapes, and trees are the structural elements of the planting design. To see how trees can be used to the best advantage, one should learn how to know them during the winter when the structural possibilities of each type of branching and silhouette can be seen. A tree can be the keynote of a garden design. As George Avery, director of the Brooklyn Botanic Garden, said, "To grow plants well is not enough. To use them well is better."

April, 1969   A.U.S.

And out of the earth made the Lord God to grow
every tree that is pleasant to the sight.
GENESIS 2:9

Trees
in a Winter
Landscape

There are fads and styles in tree planting, just as there are styles in architecture and interior decorating. It is almost possible to date a house by the type of trees planted in front of it. In Victorian times, Catalpas were popular. Sometimes they were pollarded into round balls, and sometimes the dwarf, umbrella-shaped *Catalpa bungei* was used. During the nineteen thirties, a Blue Spruce on either side of the front door was the "latest thing," and many nurseries made and lost money on that fad. Recently a symmetrical Pin Oak on the front lawn has become a status symbol in the suburbs. Chinese Elms have been recommended for their fast growth and Birch clumps for accent.

CHOOSING TREES

All of these trees are fine, but they are not always best where they are planted. Some other criteria should be used for choosing a tree than its availability and demand, and more thought should be given to its location. After all, most hardwoods live to a great age. There are Oaks living now that were small trees when the colonists first came to these shores. The Elms towering over the beautiful white houses around the commons in New England villages were planted by early settlers, and native Holly transplanted into early gardens is still thriving.

Tree planting is not something that should be done on the spur of the moment, to be redone later; a wrong choice may be regretted for years. Take time to learn something about the many beautiful trees that are available. Some live longer or grow faster. Not all trees are perfect; they have faults as well as virtues. Some trees break easily in storms or litter the ground with fruit or flowers. There are gorgeous trees that cast such heavy shade that grass is difficult to grow under the branches.

In choosing a tree, remember that the shape of the mature tree is quite different from the slim, young sapling growing in the nursery row. Like any young thing, all small trees are pretty, but trees, like people take on character as they grow older. With the help of the drawings in this book, become acquainted with the grand old trees in parks and gardens and along the roadsides. Learn the various possibilities, and find the most effective species for your needs.

It is in winter that the structural framework of the tree shows how it can best be used in the landscape. Looking at the bare skeleton and the pattern of the branches, one can see which kind of tree will be most useful in the spot where it is most needed.

VARIETIES OF TREES

Americans are very fortunate in having not only a wealth of native trees, but many more which have become naturalized on this continent. When the country was settled, plantsmen from Europe searched for new varieties to take back to the parks and gardens of Europe, while early colonists such as George Washington, who were interested in plants, imported trees from Europe. Some that were brought to America—for example the Ginkgo—had already journeyed from Asia to Europe. A Weeping Willow was one of the trees ordered for Mount Vernon along with many native species.

Later on as travel became easier, American botanists went to China and Japan and brought back many new varieties, particularly of beautiful flowering trees, such as flowering Crabapples and Cherries, and many more. Most of these trees are hardy and have become naturalized over a wide area of the United States. There is no reason for monotony in tree planting when there is such a wide variety to choose from.

Only seventy-one trees are covered in this book. Although many nurseries are limited in the kinds of trees they sell, due to local demand, there are large tree nurseries that stock almost any variety that grows. Any nearby nursery will be able to help in the quest for a special tree, if one persists. Sometimes tree companies will get native trees from the woods if they are not available any other way.

LANDSCAPING WITH TREES

BORDER

Trees have several qualities that help determine their use in landscaping. First and probably the most important is the form or shape. Visualize the shape in relationship to people and buildings. Can one walk under it or around it? Does it complement or accent a building near which it grows? Trees with horizontal branching patterns will help break tall vertical lines, while trees with more intricate branch and twig formations make interesting shadow patterns against a blank wall. Formal shapes provide accent and balance in a design.

Usually shade is a very important objective in tree planting. For this, a tree that has high, arching branches, such as an Elm, Hackberry, or Japanese Pagoda Tree, is much more satisfactory than a Pin Oak or Bald Cypress,

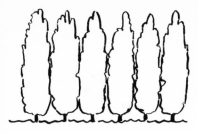

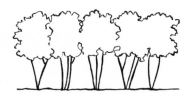

which have low branches and conical tops. A broad, spreading Weeping Willow takes up a great deal of lawn space for the amount of shade it casts, whereas a Red Oak leaves the lawn clear under its spreading branches. On a small suburban property, a group of slender trees, such as Goldenrain or Persimmon, might be more interesting and give better shade than one large tree.

Another important problem is how close to the house a tree can be planted. The wide spreading limbs of the Red Oak need plenty of space compared to the upward-reaching branches of the Sugar Maple.

Trees help to enclose areas of space with screens by formal hedges of trees of all one kind or informal hedges of masses of several different trees. Observe, when planning a screen for privacy, that those trees which start to branch high, such as the Sycamore or Tulip Tree, are not helpful as a screen or hedge. Use trees with low, spreading branches, such as the Pin Oak or Magnolia. Tall, columnar trees, such as Lombardy Poplars or Pyramidal Hornbeam, planted close together make a good screen. They also make fine accents, like exclamation points, when mixed with the more monotonous rounded or oval-shaped trees.

Trees can make space dividers, a kind of see-through screen between units of a landscape design. Redbud, Saucer Magnolia, Birch, and Yellowwood, which have multiple trunks or low, forking branches, make lovely patterned screens where complete privacy is not needed. Here the form of the trunk rather than the whole tree makes a pleasing design.

For large public buildings trees are important units of the decorative treatment because of their scale in comparison to the size of the building mass.

FORMS OF TREES

Trees grow naturally in these forms: vase-shaped; broad and spreading; oval; columnar; picturesque or irregular; pyramidal; and weeping. Then, there are some variations of these forms: round; fan-shaped; clumps or multiple stems; and horizontal branching (see table pages 6–7).

There are variations among individual trees of each species, depending on whether the tree has grown in the open or in a grove. Trees in the open have a chance to develop their natural form, while those in the woods, where they are crowded, reach up for the light and become tall and thin.

Trees are illustrated in this book in their winter forms.

5

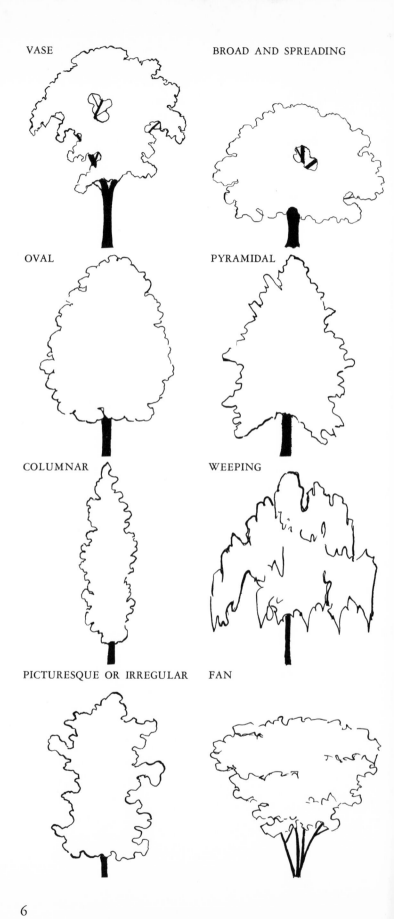

VASE

BROAD AND SPREADING

OVAL

PYRAMIDAL

COLUMNAR

WEEPING

PICTURESQUE OR IRREGULAR

FAN

6

FORMS OF TREES

VASE
Elm
Hackberry
Japanese Pagoda Tree
Silver Maple

OVAL
Sugar Maple
Cucumber Tree
Saucer Magnolia
Hawthorn
Catalpa
Beech
Black Ash
Soapberry
Horse Chestnut
Basswood
Sycamore
Persimmon

COLUMNAR
Lombardy Poplar
Gray Birch
Paper Birch
Bald Cypress
Pyramidal Hornbeam

PICTURESQUE OR IRREGULAR
Fringe Tree
Staghorn Sumac
Locust
Kentucky Coffee Tree
Ginkgo
Ailanthus
Osage Orange
Goldenrain Tree
Devil's-Walking-Stick
Shagbark Hickory
Black Gum

BROAD AND SPREADING
White Oak
Red Oak
Black Oak
White Ash
Black Walnut
Black Willow

PYRAMIDAL
Pin Oak
Tulip Tree
Sweet Gum

WEEPING
Cherry
Willow

FAN
Silk Tree
Tea Crab
Yellowwood

ROUND (not shown)
Some Hawthorns
Sargent Crab
Fringe Tree
Willow
Russian Olive
Japanese Maple
Franklin Tree

MULTIPLE-STEMMED OR
LOW-FORKED (not shown)
Birch
Redbud
Silk Tree
Yellowwood
Serviceberry
Devil's-Walking-Stick
Saucer Magnolia
Crape Myrtle
Franklin Tree
Staghorn Sumac
Fringe Tree
Smoke Tree

HORIZONTAL-BRANCHING
(not shown)
Dogwood
Black Locust
Cockspur Hawthorn
Persimmon

Many which appear as simple ovals in summer have a homely, rugged look in winter. The Weeping Cherry is a good example of a tree that changes its character in this way. In summer, the weeping characteristic is predominant, while in the winter the rugged trunk, showing up in contrast to the delicate branches, gives it a different quality of shape, which is called *picturesque.*

Interesting hybrids of many trees, such as Maple, Ash, and Cherry, have been developed in columnar form, globe-shape, and weeping varieties, thus adding greatly to the lists given here. There is no reason for monotony when nature is so lavish.

ARTIFICIAL TREE SHAPES

TOPIARY

As if nature were not lavish enough in the choice of tree shapes, man has added to natural forms by pruning and training trees into formal shapes. Topiary work— sculpturing trees and shrubs into figures or designs—was started in Roman gardens and named for a slave called Topiarius. Where owners could not afford statuary or where the climate was hard on marble figures, this type of plant pruning was popular. Evergreens are usually best for topiary work.

PLEACHING

Pleaching—interweaving tree branches to form a mass in a single plane—takes longer and is not used much today. Neither is pollarding—the cutting back of branches to the trunk to induce new growth every spring.

With smaller home gardens, however, these ancient garden practices are becoming popular again. Espaliered fruit trees fit into modern garden design against blank walls and as fences around a garden. Sculptured small trees, such as Japanese Maple, are a happy choice for container planting, and trees pleached into a flat top like a parasol make a canopy of light shade. Dogwood, Washington Thorn, Magnolia, Crabapples, and other fruits are good trees for espaliering. For pleaching Plane, Hawthorn, or Hornbeam are used.

ESPALIER

Espaliering—training trees flat against a wall or fence in symmetrical patterns—was popular in France and England, especially for fruit trees. The fruit ripened better against warm walls, and the trees took up little room in kitchen gardens. The governor's fruit garden in Colonial Williamsburg is an excellent example of an orchard in a small space, easy to care for and good to look at. There are several standard forms in this practice: gridiron; fan cordon; and U-shapes, among others.

TREE TEXTURE

The coarseness or fineness of the trunk, branches, twigs, and foliage is referred to in landscaping as texture. It is another quality that makes one tree stand out from another in the winter. Differences in texture add variety to a planting design. There are trees with very coarse texture, such as Kentucky Coffee Tree and Staghorn Sumac, and others such as Birch and Russian Olive that make a fine, delicate tracery against the sky. Some trees, such as Beech, have a massive trunk that seems fine because the bark is so smooth. The twigs and buds are also slender and graceful, so that although the Beech may grow into an enormous tree, it has a fine texture.

Coarse texture is apt to be dramatic. It shows off well planted as a point of emphasis, alone on a lawn or against rough stonework, rustic wood, or large masses of building. Stout twigs give a feeling of strength, where delicate lacy branches would seem inadequate or be completely lost from a distance. The gnarled and twisted branches of the Red Oak are picturesque as well as strong. Contrast between coarse and fine texture adds interest and character to the winter landscape particularly when snow mantles the branches. The coarser texture should be used sparingly as an accent. A good general rule to follow is about one-third coarse to two-thirds fine texture. Delicate trees such as Birch should be grown in clumps or groups where the lacy branches intermingle into a mass. Here is a list of coarse and fine textured trees:

COARSE	FINE
Kentucky Coffee Tree	Beech
Staghorn Sumac	Paper Birch
Cucumber Tree	Gray Birch
Saucer Magnolia	Russian Olive
Silk Tree	Locust
Red Oak	Weeping Willow
Black Oak	Bald Cypress
Sycamore	Hornbeam
Fringe Tree	
Ailanthus	
Horse Chestnut	
Black Walnut	
Sweet Gum	
Devil's-Walking-Stick	

TREE MASS

Another important attribute is density or mass. The density of the twigs, branches, and leaves has an effect on the wind and shade in the garden. It affects the screening ability of the tree and the clarity of the shadow patterns it will make. Trees with dense masses of twigs make a better wind barrier than those with few branches and twigs. On the other hand, where winter sun is needed near the house a Pin Oak, with its many branches and long-lasting leaves, is not as helpful in letting in sunshine as a Yellowwood.

Most trees make fairly good screens in summer, but in winter it's a different story. When the large tropical leaves fall off the Devil's-Walking-Stick or Ailanthus, there's not much screen left. The thickly interlaced branches and twigs of the Hawthorn make an impenetrable mass, and a Sugar Maple is denser than a Black Walnut.

If rugged shadow patterns against a wall or a sculptured silhouette against the sky are wanted, a tree should be picked with a branch pattern clean and bold enough to stand out and not one that is too crowded with twigs.

DENSE TREES

Hawthorn	Sweet Gum
Beech	Lombardy Poplar
Pin Oak	Birch
Sugar Maple	Hornbeam
Evergreens	Basswood

TREES THAT MAKE GOOD SHADOW PATTERNS

Staghorn Sumac	Shagbark Hickory
Redbud	Catalpa
Flowering Dogwood	Kentucky Coffee Tree
Osage Orange	Ginkgo
Fringe Tree	Tea Crab
Silk Tree	Yellowwood
Saucer Magnolia	American Elm
Red Oak	Goldenrain Tree
Black Oak	Franklin Tree
Black Walnut	

TREE COLOR

Color is the least important quality to take into consideration, although it is a most interesting one. Color changes from season to season, and in winter the colors of the trees are muted. On a day late in winter it is surprising, nevertheless, to see the variations in color from the silvery gray of the Beech to the yellow twigs of the Willow. The Black Walnut tree appears quite black, and the bark of the Paper Birch stands out sharply against evergreens. The Osage Orange has orange streaks in its bark, and the Horse Chestnut has large, glossy, brown buds. In their neutral way, all these colors are restful and beautiful in the winter garden picture.

Against a house, the choice of color of a tree in winter can be more important than it would be on the edge of a garden. A Paper Birch shows up better in winter in front of a red brick house than a white house, unless it is mixed with evergreens. One tree with a decided color, such as a Red Maple, will accent a group of trees with little winter color.

Texture does not have much influence on color. A mass of fine twigs shows as much color as a coarse branch. In general, the darker the shade of the bark, the better the pattern a tree will make against a wall.

HARDINESS OF TREES

The exact hardiness of any tree is difficult to pinpoint because it differs with exposure and altitude. A tree that grows in the South, such as a Cucumber Tree, may be found in Wiscasset, Maine, on the coast in a sheltered spot, but the same tree may not be hardy one mile from the water. Trees that are hardy at sea level may not live at altitudes several thousand feet higher up in the same area. To get right down to it, the same variety of tree may not do as well on the east and west sides of the same house. Trees that are hardy where it is cold in winter may not stand a climate such as that of Missouri where the temperature varies suddenly and there are warm spells in midwinter. In such a climate, doubtful trees should be planted on the north side or the east where they will not be warmed by the winter sun. Drought, high winds, and flooding also affect trees adversely.

It pays to check with local experts to see what is hardy in any locality, and to watch what is growing nearby. It also pays to experiment with new kinds of trees that are listed as hardy. If the early colonists and plantsmen had not tried every tree they saw or heard of, the plant list here would be much shorter. As a result of constant experiment, there is a wide choice of beautiful trees, with new varieties each year.

Descriptions
of Trees

AMERICAN ELM
Ulmus americana
size: 80–100 ft.

AMERICAN ELM
Ulmus americana

No other tree compares with the American Elm in its value as a shade tree. It was so often planted in front of the large, white colonial homes and cottages of New England that it has become a typical part of the scenery. Modern homes also nestle gratefully under its canopy of shade, and streets along which Elms were planted long ago are cool tunnels of shade in summer.

The typical vase shape of the Elm is easily identified in winter. The sturdy trunk divides 10 or 20 feet from the ground, subdivides into branches, and divides again into smaller branches. Especially in winter one can see the evenly proportioned progressive reduction from the size of the branch to the smaller branch and twig. The twigs look like feather stitching.

Because of its habit of growth with branches ascending and arching over to make a curving crown, the Elm can be planted 10 to 12 feet from a house and close to any area to be shaded. Its roots, however, may break a patio or walk if the paving is very close to the trunk. A distance of several feet should be allowed.

The Elm is a strong, dignified tree with dark gray bark broken into interlacing ridges. It will grow fairly rapidly in almost any soil. Give it enough room to spread because eventually it will grow 80 to 100 feet tall. Understory trees, such as Dogwood, will thrive in its shade. Elms grow naturally over most of the eastern half of the United States and have been planted in almost every state. In regions where ice storms are common, branches may break at the crotches, and this would spoil the effect of a formal planting temporarily or be bad for a nearby building. Otherwise, the broken branches will soon grow out again.

It is unfortunate that such a valuable tree should be bothered with several diseases and pests, including the deadly Dutch Elm-bark beetle. Everything is being done that can be done to find a remedy and save the existing Elms. In the meantime it would be best to choose the disease-resistant hybrids, of which Christine Buisman (*Ulmus carpinifolia*) is the best.

HACKBERRY
Celtis occidentalis
size: 80–120 ft.

HACKBERRY
Celtis occidentalis

At a quick glance, a Hackberry might be mistaken for an Elm, to which it is related. The size and shape are quite similar, but the crown of the Hackberry is more ragged and not as symmetrical. In winter, it is easy to distinguish because of a disease called *witches' brooms* which disfigures the slender branches with clusters of twigs. This disease is caused by a fungus and is considered ornamental by many people. Another easy mark of identification is the bark. It is light gray-brown with tight ridges which are not continuous and sometimes roughened by irregular wart-shaped galls. A gall is a small bump caused by an insect or fungus. When the tree becomes old the bark smooths out over the well-shaped trunk. In fact, the older a Hackberry grows the most beautiful it becomes. They may reach a height of 120 feet.

The Hackberry should be planted as a shade tree where the Dutch Elm beetle is causing havoc, since it has the same basic shape and makes as good an umbrella of shade as the Elm. From a landscaping point of view, it does not do as well as an Elm where a perfect form is required, because of its unsymmetrical top.

Bird lovers like Hackberry trees because the birds enjoy the purple cherrylike fruit that hangs on long stalks during the winter. They also eat the galls made on the foliage during the summer by several insect pests. The diseases which affect this tree do not seem to do much damage.

The Hackberry tree is commonly found over a wide range from the Atlantic to the Rockies. It will tolerate various soils and will even stand short periods of flooding without harm.

AMERICAN BEECH
Fagus americana
size: 60–120 ft.

A full-grown Beech is a massive tree and yet, for all its size, an elegant one. Everything about it is fine from the beautiful tips of the long, tapering buds to the satin-smooth bark around its sturdy trunk. In the open, a Beech tree has a wide, spreading, rounded head with many long, smooth, horizontal branches starting quite low on the trunk and sometimes sweeping the ground. The upper branches ascend.

Because of its wide spread, a Beech should grow out on an open lawn where it can be enjoyed from all sides. It will grow close to other trees, but then it will be taller and not so wide, with branches that start higher on the trunk. Beech trees are slow-growing. They stand shearing well and make excellent tall hedges where there is room. Since the old leaves hang on the tree late into the winter, Beech is good for screening.

An interesting characteristic of the Beech is the way in which the slender, angled twigs grow more densely along the outer edges of the branches making a unique ruffled appearance when seen from a distance in the winter. The Beech also stands out noticeably in winter because of the silvery, grayish-blue, satin-smooth bark which stretches tightly around the trunk from the buttressed roots to the branches. As the tree becomes older, the bark is marked with irregular, darker bands. The bark of the Purple Beech, *Fagus sylvatica atropurpurea,* is a deeper gray.

Beeches are hardy over the eastern third of the United States, south to the Gulf. They live long, and some have been found 120 feet high with trunks 4 feet in diameter. They are among our best ornamental trees.

AMERICAN BASSWOOD
Tilia americana
size: 70–90 ft.

AMERICAN BASSWOOD
Tilia americana

The American Basswood is another handsome shade tree, tall and compact with a narrow, rounded crown and a formal oval shape. At first glance from a distance in winter, the numerous slender branches may remind one of a Sugar Maple. A closer look, however, shows several very different characteristics. On the lower part of the tree, the branches droop gracefully, turning up on the ends, and the woody, pealike fruit hangs in clusters from a stalk ending in a narrow leaf like a wing. These are quite different from the fruit of any other tree.

The American Basswood is often called the American Linden or Lime. It grows fast and makes a beautiful ornamental shade tree because of its symmetrical habit of growth. It should be planted on an open lawn where the low, hanging branches of the mature tree will not be disturbed. Since the foliage is thick, Basswoods make a good screen or background. The European variety *Tilia europea vulgaris* is often planted as a street tree. The Little Leaf Linden, *Tilia cordata,* is a smaller-sized tree. It is also the hardiest and will withstand city conditions.

On young Basswood trees the bark is smooth and grayish. As the tree matures, the bark becomes deeply furrowed into firm, vertical ridges with horizontal cracks.

Basswood is distributed over most of the eastern part of the United States from Canada south, except for the coastal regions from Delaware south to around the Gulf. It will grow on the Pacific slope. Under average conditions, the Basswood will grow 70 to 90 feet tall. Deep, moist soil suits it best.

TWIG DETAILS

AMERICAN ELM

HACKBERRY

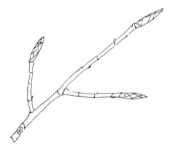

AMERICAN BEECH

AMERICAN BASSWOOD

Notice how the twigs on the Elm stand out alternately along the small branches. They are slender, reddish brown in color. The pointed, smooth buds are lighter brown, with dark-edged scales.

Hackberry twigs are not as regular in progression along the branches as are Elm twigs. They are slender, light brown in color when the tree is young, and gray when the tree is mature. The buds are small and triangular in shape with hairy scales. The end bud is false; that is, the end bud is shed and a side bud acts as an end bud.

Like the rest of this tree, the brownish gray twigs are elegant and slender. The buds are narrow, about an inch long, and taper to a point. They are encased in shiny, brown scales. Each leaf scar is encircled by stipule scars. These are usually in pairs made by a growth at the base of the leaf stalk, caused when the leaves fall off.

The moderately thick twigs of the Basswood are red or green. The buds appear alternately in a zigzag fashion. They are pointed, fat, egg-shaped, and shiny red with two scales. The coloring of twigs and buds intensifies as spring comes on. There is no true terminal bud.

NORTHERN RED OAK
Quercus rubra
size: 70–90 ft.

NORTHERN RED OAK
Quercus rubra

Notice a noble and picturesque tree that makes a spread wider than it is high, and it is apt to be a Northern Red Oak. This is one of the most beautiful and largest of the Oaks. It will grow 70 to 90 feet tall, and the diameter of its spread is even greater. The massive, stout trunk separates into several large limbs that radiate out from the trunk. They twist in angular lines and slant gently upwards. Even the twigs are twisted. Young trees are apt to look irregular and misshapen, but that is part of their homely quality. Many times they are passed over in the nursery in favor of a more symmetrical tree. Here it pays to know how grand the mature tree can be.

Although the branches cover a large area, they start out higher on the trunk than those of the Pin Oak, so that the tree makes effective shade. This is the kind of tree around which a garden should be planned. It would be ideal to shade a patio or in the center of a circular drive. Because the Oak holds onto its leaves late into the winter, it would not let the winter sun shine into the house if it were planted in front of a window. The branches will hold a swing or a hammock. The whole tree has a rugged look that fits in well with stone and contemporary wooden buildings. Red Oaks will grow under city conditions, and they are the fastest growing of all Oaks. Plant an acorn, and soon there will be a tree.

These Oaks are strong and durable in storms and practically free from insects and disease. In its natural range from the Canadian border south through Arkansas and Tennessee, the Northern Red Oak grows best in deep, well-drained soil.

PIN OAK
Quercus palustris

The Pin Oak is a very popular, specimen lawn tree for many reasons. Nurserymen like it because it transplants easily, with its fibrous root system, and because it is comparatively free of insects. Home owners are pleased with its quick growth, neat habits, and glossy foliage. It will stand city smoke and does not break easily in storms.

This tree can be identified in winter with no trouble because it differs from other oaks in three ways. First, the trunk is straight with branches that are slender for an oak, even when the tree is old. Second, the shape of the tree is pyramidal and symmetrical, with lower branches sweeping toward the ground, middle ones extending straight out, and the top branches slanting up. The branches are covered with many short spur or pinlike twigs from which the tree gets its name. The dead brown leaves hang on most of the winter.

Because of its shape, it is not the best shade tree. Pin Oaks make good specimen trees and are excellent where formality is wanted, perhaps one tree on either side of a walk in front of a building or as a row in a park. They fit in well around modern buildings. Since Pin Oaks are dense both in winter and summer, they make good background trees for hiding a poor view. The fine texture of the grayish brown bark, with tight, low, scaly ridges and the neat, shiny leaves, contribute to its formal look.

As Oaks go, the Pin Oak is a moderate-sized tree, reaching 50 to 70 feet and covering an area 30 to 40 feet wide. In its native habitat, it is found in poorly drained flats or clay ridges across the center of the eastern half of the United States from lower New England to the center of North Carolina. The Pin Oak adapts itself well to the average lawn.

BLACK OAK
Quercus velutina
size: 50–60 ft.

BLACK OAK
Quercus velutina

The Black Oak is not often planted as an ornamental tree, but it is well worth treasuring for its picturesque beauty and rugged qualities if it is already growing on a site. Like most other Oaks, it needs plenty of room to develop. The Black Oak is not always easy to distinguish from other Oaks in the winter because it varies in form in different localities of its wide range, which covers most of the eastern United States.

It is helpful in identifying this tree in winter to look for its wide, irregular crown and large branches that slant upwards. In comparison, the twigs are quite light. The tree in the illustration is from the Maine coast. Here the tree seems to personify the rugged terrain and show the ocean winds in its stout twisted branches. In poor soil such as this, the trunk tapers and the limbs branch out low. In good soil, the trunk grows straight up with little taper, and the branches start higher up. In that case, it looks more like a Scarlet Oak with heavier branches. The bark is dark, almost black, and has deep, rough, blocky furrows. Along the coast, the color of the bark is lighter.

One of the disadvantages of this Oak is the gradual dying back of large branches, which have to be cut off. It will not tolerate shade, but does not mind drought because of the deep tap root which anchors it. These Oaks grow fairly fast and reach a height of 60 feet or more, with an 80 foot spread. They will live one hundred fifty years or more.

WHITE OAK
Quercus alba

The dignified and stately White Oak is a beautiful tree in winter. It is one of the best loved and most common Oaks in the eastern United States. Children can swing on the massive, horizontal, lower limbs. The gnarled, ascending, upper branches give it a beautifully proportioned, round crown. In winter, the light gray bark on the sturdy trunk is a distinguishing characteristic. The bark has scaly plates and shallow fissures. In contrast, the stout twigs are smooth. They are greenish red.

Since these Oaks spread 60 feet or more, they are not suitable for small city lots and should not be planted too close to a building. If there is a White Oak growing on a piece of property, guard it as the treasure it is. Do not cut or fill around it. Money cannot buy these trees in large sizes. They should be planted young at a 6- to 8-foot size. White Oaks grow slowly and live to an impressive age. Other, fast-growing, shorter-lived trees could be planted in the vicinity while the more valuable tree was making progress.

The dried, brown leaves persist on the tree late into the winter, adding a pleasing warmth to the scene. The color and texture of the White Oak looks well with contemporary wood or stone buildings. It will tolerate a variety of growing conditions but does not grow in northern Maine, in Florida, or the Gulf Coast.

TWIG DETAILS

NORTHERN RED OAK

PIN OAK

BLACK OAK

WHITE OAK

On the Red Oak the slender, smooth, green to reddish brown twigs have conical buds three-eighths to five-eighths of an inch long. The buds are reddish brown and fringed with hair. Alternate buds cluster near the end bud. The acorn cup is flat and saucer-shaped.

The short, spurlike twigs of the Pin Oak are slender. In winter they are red-brown. The numerous smooth buds are egg-shaped and pointed. The end buds are small and sharp. The small acorns have flat saucerlike cups.

The fairly thick twigs of the Black Oak are dull red-brown with large breathing pores, or lenticels. The buds are sharply angled and coated with matted hair. At the ends of the twigs, the alternate, yellow-gray, sharply pointed buds cluster about the terminal bud. The acorn cups are bowl shaped with fringelike scales that extend more than halfway up the nut.

It is characteristic of Oak-tree buds to cluster at the end of the twig. White Oak buds are small, bluntly egg-shaped, and have smooth, red-brown scales. The twigs are greenish red in color. Acorn cups cover a third of the long acorn.

SUGAR MAPLE
Acer saccharum

The silhouette of the Sugar Maple in winter shows a short trunk and many branches ascending at quite a steep angle to form a perfect, rounded, oval crown. The branches are opposite one another. The bushy effect made by the branches and fine, small twigs has given the tree the nickname of Sugar Bush. In early spring when the snow begins to melt and the sap starts to rise, the sweet sap taken from the Sugar Maple is made into maple syrup and sugar.

Often Sugar Maples were planted along roadsides and in front of colonial homes where their dignified forms make beautiful patterns against the winter sky. They are rather formal trees, always regular in shape. They grow slowly into large trees, eventually reaching 70 to 100 feet in height, and they need room to develop. On large-scale properties, they would make a fine screen planting.

Young trees have a smooth, silvery bark, which later becomes a dark gray and breaks up into hard, flinty flakes. Sometimes the bark is deeply grooved.

These Maples are popular for landscaping, not only for their beauty of form, but also for the brilliant fall coloring of red and gold. They transplant easily. It is difficult to grow grass under a Sugar Maple because the roots are so near the surface of the ground and the shade is dense. Other ground covers will do very well, however. They will not tolerate city conditions. Sugar Maples grow in every state east of the plains except Florida and are most prevalent in New England and the Appalachian Mountains.

SILVER MAPLE
Acer saccharinum
size: 60–80 ft.

SILVER MAPLE
Acer saccharinum

When seen at a distance the shape of the Silver Maple is very much like that of the American Elm, with several large branches spreading up and out to make a broad, arching crown. Close by, the differences show up, however. First of all, the drooping outer branches are thicker than the graceful Elm branches, and they curl up on the ends like fishhooks. Also the branches are opposite one another. There are three tree families that have opposite branches, the Maples, Ashes, and Horse Chestnut.

Where the Silver Maple grows in the open, the trunk is quite short and heavy with low-forking branches. The bark of the young Maple is silver-gray and smooth, and the color stays silver as the tree matures and the bark breaks into thin, flaky scales.

This Maple is often called the Soft Maple. It grows very fast and becomes a large tree 60 to 80 feet tall. Because of the fast growth and wide spread of the branches, the branches are weak and will break under an accumulation of snow and ice or a strong wind. Since it grows quickly, the Silver Maple is very popular in housing developments where shade is needed, but one should be careful to plant it away from wires or buildings that might be harmed by broken branches.

The Silver Maple transplants easily. The roots are shallow and spreading. There is a fungus disease which causes heart rot, and many old trees are hollow. They do not have any distinct fall coloring. Silver Maples are hardy over the eastern half of the United States, although they are rarely found growing naturally along the seacoast.

BLACK ASH
Fraxinus nigra
size: 40–50 ft.

BLACK ASH
Fraxinus nigra

The stout twigs of the Black Ash make crosses against the sky in winter. This is the one tree among the Ashes, Maples, and Horse Chestnuts, which all have opposite branches, where the habit shows up very clearly in winter. The Black Ash has a straight, columnar trunk and slender, ascending branches. The head is narrow, rounded, and rather open. Often the branches start high on the trunk. It is a small or medium-sized tree, growing about 40 to 50 feet and is fast growing.

This tree is also called the Swamp Ash and the Basket Ash. It is commonly found in swamps and near slow-running streams. The Black Ash would be useful as a shade tree only if there is a site in the garden where the soil is wet, perhaps by a pond. Since most trees do not like wet feet, it is good to have one that does. It is nice planted in groups.

The Indians used the wood from this tree to make baskets. They beat the wood with mallets until it split into thin sheets which could be cut into strips. Today we make woven chair seats out of it.

The bark of the Black Ash is smoother than the bark of the other Ash trees. It is ash-gray with tight, scaly ridges, which are powdery when rubbed.

The Black Ash grows in the northern states, west to South Dakota and south to Iowa and Virginia. Further south, the Green Ash (*Fraxinus pennsylvanica*), which is very similar, has been planted extensively as a shade tree. It has prominent green twigs in the winter. It also grows very fast.

WHITE ASH
Fraxinus americana
size: 70–80 ft.

WHITE ASH
Fraxinus americana

The White Ash is tall, stately, and dignified. Trees 70 to 80 feet tall are common among this largest of the Ashes. Giants of the species grow in the fertile soil of the Ohio River valley. It has a strong, usually straight trunk and a broad, rounded head. The thick branches grow opposite to one another. The sturdy twigs show this opposite trait predominantly when the leaves are gone in winter, although the twigs curve somewhat and do not make crosses as those of the Black Ash do. The White Ash shows up beautifully in the winter landscape and the strong branches wear snow easily without bending.

The bark is rich and dignified, ash-gray in color. On old trees, it becomes very thick and deeply divided by narrow, diamond-shaped furrows into flat ridges.

While the majority of trees have both male (staminate) and female (pistillate) flowers on the same tree, most of the Ash trees have male and female flowers on separate trees. This trait shows up in winter especially on the White Ash, where the female tree is literally covered with clusters of paddle-shaped seeds.

Plant a White Ash where it will have room to develop into a handsome shade tree. It is especially admired in the fall for its purple and gold coloring. This Ash, the finest of all the native Ashes, grows all over the eastern third of the United States except in coastal areas south from New Jersey and around the Gulf. It is easy to transplant.

TWIG DETAILS

SUGAR MAPLE

SILVER MAPLE

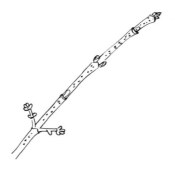

BLACK ASH

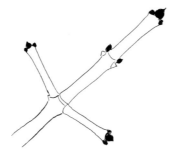

WHITE ASH

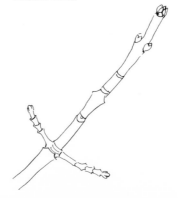

The twigs are slender and pale reddish brown in winter, with sharp-pointed, pale-brown buds that have numerous scales. The terminal bud is only about one-quarter inch long, and the side buds are smaller.

The blunt buds of the Silver Maple give off a disagreeable odor when they are crushed. The buds at the end of the twigs are one-fourth of an inch long and have three or four pairs of bud scales. Buds along the sides have short stalks and are usually accompanied by shiny flower buds. The twigs are a greenish orange, shading to brown and red.

The sturdy twigs of this tree are smooth and colored a pale, grayish olive-green. In contrast, the buds are dark, almost black. The end bud is much larger than the side buds. It is egg-shaped with a pointed tip.

The curving twigs of the White Ash are thick. They are gray-green in color, sometimes tinged with maroon on the surface. The terminal buds are dark and rounded. When the leaves fall, semicircular leaf scars are left on the twig. They differ in size and shape on each tree and are one of the means of identification (see also twig detail of female White Ash, page 51).

RED MAPLE
Acer rubrum
size: 40–50 ft.

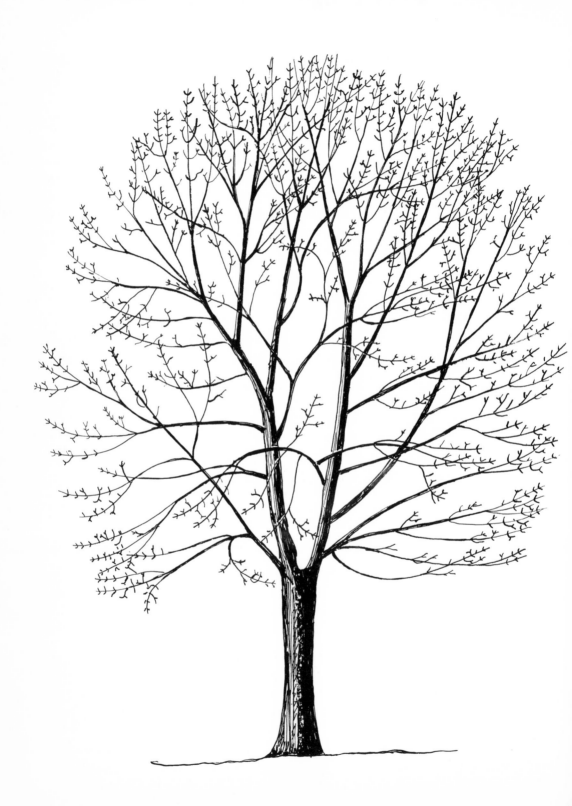

When the winter sun shines on the bright red twigs of the Red Maple, it is easy to distinguish from other trees. It is aptly named because there is some bright red color on the tree at any season.

In the open, this tree has a short trunk with a dense, oval crown. The branches curve upward. It is usually a moderate-sized tree from 40 to 50 feet tall, although larger specimens are found in favorable growing areas. It is also known as Swamp Maple, and it thrives in any moist, fertile soil.

In winter, the smooth, silver-gray bark of the young tree is similar to the bark of the Beech, but the opposite-growing branches and the red twigs make the total effect of the Red Maple quite different. As the tree grows older, the bark darkens to a deeper gray, with shallow fissures and long, flaky ridges. The fissures are much shallower than those on the bark of the Sugar Maple.

The shape, size, and beauty of the Red Maple make it a desirable shade tree for the average-sized home if there is plenty of moisture. Plant one where it can be enjoyed from a window. A line of Red Maples along a street is a gallant sight. They show off especially when mixed with evergreens, where the pale gray bark and red twigs make a winter contrast. There is a columnar variety, *Acer rubrum* var. *columnare,* which should be used more often when a vertical accent is needed. A row of them would make a good screen all year. The Red Maple is not as hard on the grass beneath it as the other varieties of Maple, perhaps because it likes so much moisture.

This Maple grows in lowlands and swamps from Canada south to Texas, over the eastern half of the United States. It is best to transplant it in the fall because of its early blooming period.

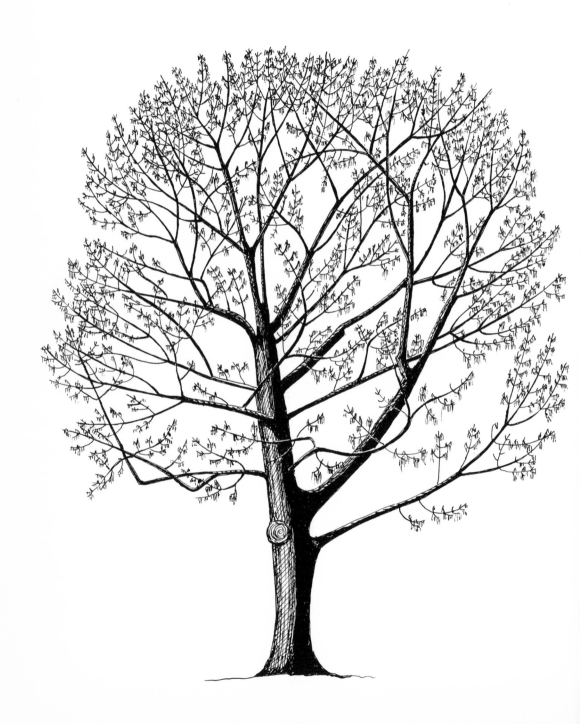

BOX ELDER
Acer negundo

The Box Elder tree belongs to the Maple family. It is sometimes called the Ash-Leaved Maple and is probably planted least of all the Maples as an ornamental tree. It has a short, crooked trunk dividing into several stout, spreading branches, with an open unsymmetrical rounded crown. The trees vary in shape and should not be planted where formality is required. It is a casual tree with a homely air, a good tree for children to climb.

In winter, the opposite twigs of the Box Elder are a glowing olive-green that warms up the landscape. Like the White Ash, this tree has its staminate (male) and pistillate (female) flowers on separate trees, although the other Maples do not. A female tree is literally covered with drooping clusters of V-shaped, winged seeds hanging down 6 to 8 inches. These seeds stay on the tree most of the winter, looking like straw-colored Wisteria. When the wind blows the seeds away, the stems are left behind.

The bark varies from yellowish green on young trees to a dark grayish brown on older trees. It is thin with shallow, narrow, topped ridges.

The Box Elder is a very hardy tree. It will tolerate extremes of temperature and soil conditions. It grows very fast to a height of 40 to 50 feet. Because of this it is helpful as a shade tree where conditions are difficult. Box Elder bugs infest these trees periodically. They do not seem to hurt the trees, but they can be a nuisance to a nearby house.

Box Elders grow wild throughout most of the United States, from the eastern slopes of the Rockies to the Atlantic seaboard.

MORAINE LOCUST
Gleditsia triacanthos inermis var. *moraine*
size: 50–75 ft.

MORAINE LOCUST
Gleditsia triacanthos inermis
var. *moraine*

Hybridizers have been busy trying to find trees that will grow in the beautiful vase shape of the American Elm. The Moraine Locust is a patented hybrid of the Thornless Honey Locust, which has a similar spreading shape. The other growth habits, however, are quite different and show up especially in the winter. The crown is flatter than that of the Elm and more open. The short trunk divides into several upward-spreading limbs with numerous, somewhat horizontal branches. The stout twigs have a distinctive zigzag pattern that gives the tree a stiff look in winter compared to the graceful drooping effect of the outer Elm branches.

Because of its attractive shape, rapid growth, and easy transplantability, the Moraine Locust and other patented hybrids of the Thornless Honey Locust have become very popular as shade trees around modern homes. Locusts thrive in poor soil. They would do well in newly developed areas where the ground has been filled or the top soil bulldozed off. They stand city conditions well also. In areas where ice storms are prevalent, they might split and break at the crotches.

On young trees, the bark is almost smooth and greenish brown in color. As the tree matures the bark becomes very dark, with longitudinal fissures and wide, deep ridges.

The Honey Locust is found in the central part of the United States, from the Appalachian Mountains west to Nebraska and Texas.

TWIG DETAILS

RED MAPLE

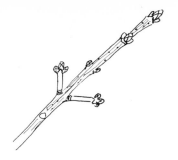

BOX ELDER

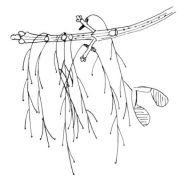

MORAINE LOCUST

FEMALE WHITE ASH

The slender twigs of the Red Maple are bright, shiny red and dotted with small, pale breathing pores, or lenticels. The blunt, oval, opposite buds are also red, with up to four visible scales. The scars left behind by the fallen leaves are crescent-shaped.

The stout Box Elder twigs are olive-green. The blunt, oval buds are covered with white, woolly down. The terminal bud is larger than the side buds, and the tips of the scars made by the fallen leaves meet at a sharp angle.

The zigzag twigs of this locust show up well at a distance. The buds are indistinct, buried in the smooth, shiny, reddish brown bark, with only the tips showing. The leaf scars are U-shaped.

The twigs of the female tree have clusters of paddle-shaped tan seeds that last late into the fall. When they blow off they leave wiry brown stalks that persist all winter.

HORSE CHESTNUT
Aesculus hippocastanum
size: 50–80 ft.

HORSE CHESTNUT
Aesculus hippocastanum

The Horse Chestnut was introduced into the United States early in the eighteenth century from Europe, although it came originally from Asia. It belongs to the same family as the Ohio Buckeye, and its winter form is much the same.

Because of its smooth, oval outline and showy, white blossoms, the Horse Chestnut has been planted in every state in the union. In winter, it is a study in sturdy symmetry with its orderly arrangement of ascending branches. The branches have a gentle, reverse curve that is unique. They turn up on the ends, which are tipped with huge, glossy, conical buds. This is one of the three species with branches that grow opposite one another, but the trait is not always noticeable from a distance.

The Horse Chestnut grows into a relatively large tree, 50 to 80 feet tall, but so compact that it does not take up much room on a lawn. All the details of the branches, twigs, and buds are large yet elegant in form. When the leaves are gone, the design of the branches against the sky or a building has the effect of a piece of sculpture. Snow lying on the thick branches enhances the picture.

Plant this tree where the silhouette can be seen. Think of it not only as a superb shade tree but also as a garden ornament. It will always attract attention.

The bark is colored dull brownish black and breaks into large, scaly plates with shallow fissures between.

AILANTHUS
Ailanthus glandulosa

The Ailanthus is commonly called by its oriental name Tree of Heaven, alluding to its ultimate height of 80 to 100 feet under ideal conditions. It was brought to this country early in the eighteenth century from England, where it was first introduced from China. It was also called Chinese Sumac, because the leaves are similar.

This tree has a homely, rugged style in the winter, with an irregular, flat-topped crown. The branches reach upwards like raised arms. The sparse twigs curve up along the branches at intervals in ragged scallops. The texture of the whole tree is coarse and rough and very distinctive. The Ailanthus looks well with modern architecture, giving a sculptured effect to the planting in winter. It is one tree that has the same texture in all seasons. Since individual trees vary in form, they will not do for a formal planting. The gray bark has shallow, lengthwise fissures that are lighter in color than the regular ridges.

Ailanthus will grow under adverse conditions of hard, sunbaked soil and city smoke and gases. It is hardy from New York south. In the East, it has escaped cultivation to become almost a weed. In the West, it still grows only locally, where it has been planted. There are two things to watch out for in planting an Ailanthus: first it spreads from the roots and sends up suckers; secondly this species has separate trees for male and female flowers, and only the female tree should be planted. The flowers of the male tree have a very unpleasant odor. The male and female trees can be distinguished by the flowers in summer. In cases where one sex is objectionable, the trees grown by nurserymen are propagated by cuttings, so that only desirable trees are sold.

GINKGO
Ginkgo biloba

This unusual tree was brought originally from China by steps to Japan, England, and then America. It was found in the temple gardens of China and Japan. The name *Ginkgo* is Chinese and means silver fruit. It is also called Maidenhair Fern Tree, because of the shape of the leaves. The Ginkgo is one of the few known trees that go back to prehistoric times.

The distinctive shape of the Ginkgo shows its relationship to the conifers. The trunk is straight and tapered, and the branches are arranged in whorls, that is, in a circle about the trunk. The lower branches have a slight slant upwards, while the upper ones ascend more steeply, so that the whole tree has a pyramidal look when it is young. As it grows older, the crown becomes more open and irregular. The winter silhouette is clean looking and not cluttered up with a multitude of twigs. Along the small branches are spurlike shoots from which the clusters of leaves grow. The Ginkgo makes a distinctive ornamental tree for any garden. It is handsome when planted in front of large buildings. There is a columnar variety, *Ginkgo biloba* var. *fastigiata* which is very striking.

Ginkgo trees grow slowly to a height of 60 to 80 feet. They live to be very old. The bark is thick and ash-gray. The narrow, longitudinal ridges are separated by shallow fissures.

Ginkgos thrive on fertile soil, but they will tolerate city growing conditions. No diseases or pests bother this tree. There are separate male and female trees. Only the male tree should be planted, because the fruit on the female tree has an objectionable odor and becomes slippery when it falls to the ground. Nurserymen do not sell female Ginkgo trees for that reason. Trees are grown from cuttings to assure proper sex.

LOMBARDY POPLAR
Populus nigra var. *italica*

The Lombardy Poplar was introduced into this country from Europe long ago. Mention of the name brings the picture of a tall, very slim tree to mind. Its distinctive, narrow, columnar form is easily recognized at any time of year. In winter, the characteristic vertical branches can be seen. The trunk is straight and tapering. Near the bottom, the vertically slanting branches begin growing in layers, so that the outline of the tree has a wavy appearance as one layer stops and another begins.

The shape of this tree and the small amount of room it takes up have made it popular in gardening as a tall screen. It also makes an arresting accent. The new twigs have a yellowish color that is warming in the winter landscape. Bark on an older tree has deep furrows and a grayish brown color.

Lombardy Poplars grow very fast, reaching a height of 30 to 50 feet in a relatively short time. As trees go, however, it is not a long-lived tree. It is hardy in most parts of the United States. The roots spread over a large area and starve nearby plants. There are columnar forms of other, slower growing trees, such as Red Maple, Cherry, and Ginkgo, to mention a few, that would make better ornamental trees for vertical accents.

TWIG DETAILS　　　　HORSE CHESTNUT

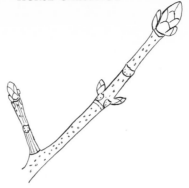

AILANTHUS

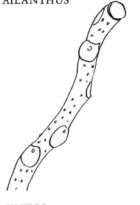

GINKGO

LOMBARDY POPLAR

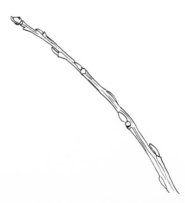

The heavy twigs of the Horse Chestnut have large, reddish brown end buds covered with a sticky gum. On either side of the end bud is a smaller side bud. Below the opposite leaf buds along the stems are large, horseshoe-shaped scars where last year's leaves fell off. These scars help give the tree its name. There are many lenticels.

The yellow-brown twigs of the Ailanthus are very thick. They have false end buds, that is, buds which do not develop. The buds are tiny and woolly, set above very large, shield-shaped leaf scars. The lenticels or breathing pores are conspicuous.

A definite zigzag makes the Ginkgo twigs easy to identify. Stubby, spurlike shoots with thickly clustered leaf scars are also characteristic of this tree. The chestnut-brown buds are short and conelike on grayish brown twigs.

The Lombardy Poplar has smooth, slender, light tan-colored twigs, against which are pressed the pointed, shiny, greenish brown buds. The buds have several scales.

BLACK WILLOW
Salix nigra
size: 30–50 ft.

BLACK WILLOW
Salix nigra

This is the most common of all the native Willows and one of the largest. It grows 30 to 50 feet high or more along the banks of streams, rivers, and ponds from Canada west to North Dakota and south to Texas. Usually the trunks lean outward over the water, or clusters of Willows lean out from each other. The trunks are often crooked. In winter, the distinction between the heavy trunk with upward-growing limbs and the delicate branches with fine twigs stands out.

The broad, flat-topped head of the Willow is irregular and open. Willow wood is weak and brittle. Often branches break off, and clusters of new shoots give the tree a ragged appearance. The whole tree has a shaggy look. The only use of the Black Willow in landscaping is as a stabilizer of banks by water, where its wide, interlacing root system holds the soil from washing away. In this habitat they look natural.

The rough, deep-furrowed bark is blackish brown with broad interlacing ridges that appear shaggy and loose. Willows sprout easily from cuttings.

WEEPING WILLOW
Salix babylonica
size: 30–50 ft.

WEEPING WILLOW
Salix babylonica

The famous, beloved Blue Willoware china was named for this Willow which grew originally in China and Asia. The long, gracefully drooping branches have been a symbol of grief in many songs and stories.

No other tree has quite the same lovely form as the Weeping Willow. The broad, round crown and the swaying, pendulous terminal branches are distinctive. They give the tree a restful look compared to the dynamic forms of other trees. As with other Willows, the trunk and limbs of the Weeping Willow are bulky in comparison to the very slender branches and twigs. The terminal branches hang down in lengths up to 10 feet. Although they look supple as they sway in the breeze, they are brittle and break easily. When the sap comes up in the early spring, the yellow color of the twigs brightens, and the bare tree gives a warm, sunny effect.

This is a dignified tree, for all its grace, because of its large mass. As a lawn tree, it takes up a great deal of room, since the lower branches sweep the ground. Where there is room, it makes a beautiful ornamental tree, a good background for solid objects, such as sculpture, or dense plants, such as evergreens. Willows like moisture, and a Weeping Willow is just right by a pond, but they will do well on a lawn also. The roots of this tree have a bad tendency to clog sewer and drainage pipes, so plant a Willow well away from any drainage systems.

STAGHORN SUMAC
Rhus typhina
size: 15–30 ft.

STAGHORN SUMAC
Rhus typhina

The name Staghorn gives a good picture of this small tree in winter. The thick, upcurving, velvety branches and twigs look very much like the antlers of a deer. The dense clusters of hairy, dark red fruit, borne in spikes on the ends of the branches, remain on the tree all winter. It is an easy tree to identify because of its distinctive habits of growth.

The shape of the Staghorn Sumac is unsymmetrical and somewhat flat topped. The rugged and often crooked branches start forking low on the trunk. They are clean and uncluttered with very few twigs, so that this Sumac does not make a good screen in winter. The heavy, curving branches do make a definite and emphatic pattern against a wall. The tree is useful in landscaping for its dramatic impact both winter and summer. It also looks well in a natural, informal setting by a stone wall or behind a split-rail fence. A thicket of Sumac on a barren hillside is spectacular when the leaves turn flaming red.

In the northern part of its range, from the Canadian border south, the Staghorn Sumac is usually a shrub. It becomes larger as it grows further south into Mississippi and Alabama and may grow into a small tree 30 feet in height. Sumacs will grow in poor soil. They spread rapidly by underground roots and may become a nuisance.

DEVIL'S-WALKING-STICK
Aralia spinosa
size: 10–30 ft.

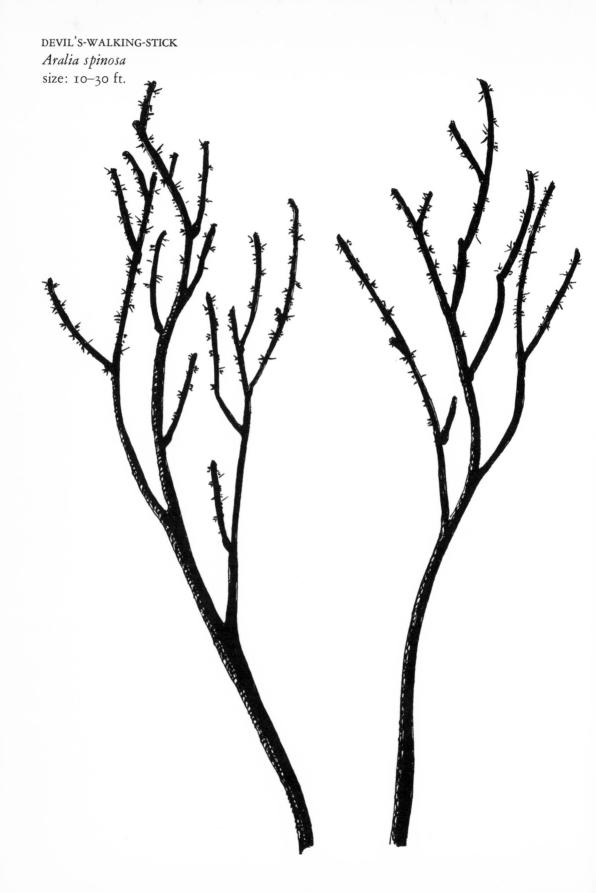

DEVIL'S-WALKING-STICK
Aralia spinosa

Stick is certainly a descriptive name for these spiny specimens. In winter, they are hardly beautiful, rather grotesque, as they stand stiff and gaunt with either no branches or very few thick, stubby ones curving steeply up. Another name for this peculiar tree is Hercules'-Club. During the early part of the winter, large heads of purple berries on red stalks make quite a show at the tops of the Sticks.

Since the slender trunks with brown bark are so spiny, they should be planted where there is no traffic. They would be good for filling in a corner where quick growth and moderate height are needed. Against a high, blank wall, their bare winter and tropical summer silhouettes are dramatic. As a focal plant in a modern garden with a gravel mulch around it, one would be unique.

Devil's-Walking-Stick grows in the Southern states and as far north as Pennsylvania and Missouri. Where it is not hardy, it freezes to the ground and comes up anew each year, growing quickly from 10 to 15 feet high. In the South, it will grow into a tree 30 feet tall or more. There is a Chinese variety, the Chinese Angelica Tree (*Aralia chinensis* var. *elata*) that has few spines and is hardier. These are quick-growing trees. The native varieties have a habit of spreading from the roots, and it may be that all of the species have the same habit.

TWIG DETAILS   BLACK WILLOW

WEEPING WILLOW

STAGHORN SUMAC

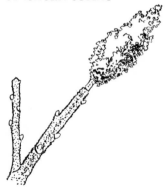

DEVIL'S-WALKING-STICK

The slender Black Willow twigs are smooth and greenish in color, becoming reddish as they mature. They are quite brittle at the base. The small, long, pointed buds have a single scale, which is a shiny reddish brown color, covering the entire bud.

Small, smooth, pointed buds lie flat alternately along the greenish yellow twigs of the Weeping Willow. The leaf scars are inconspicuous. As the twig becomes older, it is a lustrous, light tan, and the buds are bright reddish brown.

This Sumac's large, round twigs are velvet brown. Even the small, conical buds are covered with velvety hairs. The leaf scars are C-shaped, nearly encircling the buds. The compact, conical clusters of fruit, 5 to 8 inches long, stay on the tree all winter. They are densely covered with bright red hairs.

The prickles scattered at intervals, particularly beneath the leaf scars, make this very stout twig a Devil's-Walking-Stick indeed. The flat, triangular buds are chestnut-brown. The leaf scars go halfway around the twig. There is a terminal bud.

TULIP TREE
Liriodendron tulipifera
size: 80–150 ft.

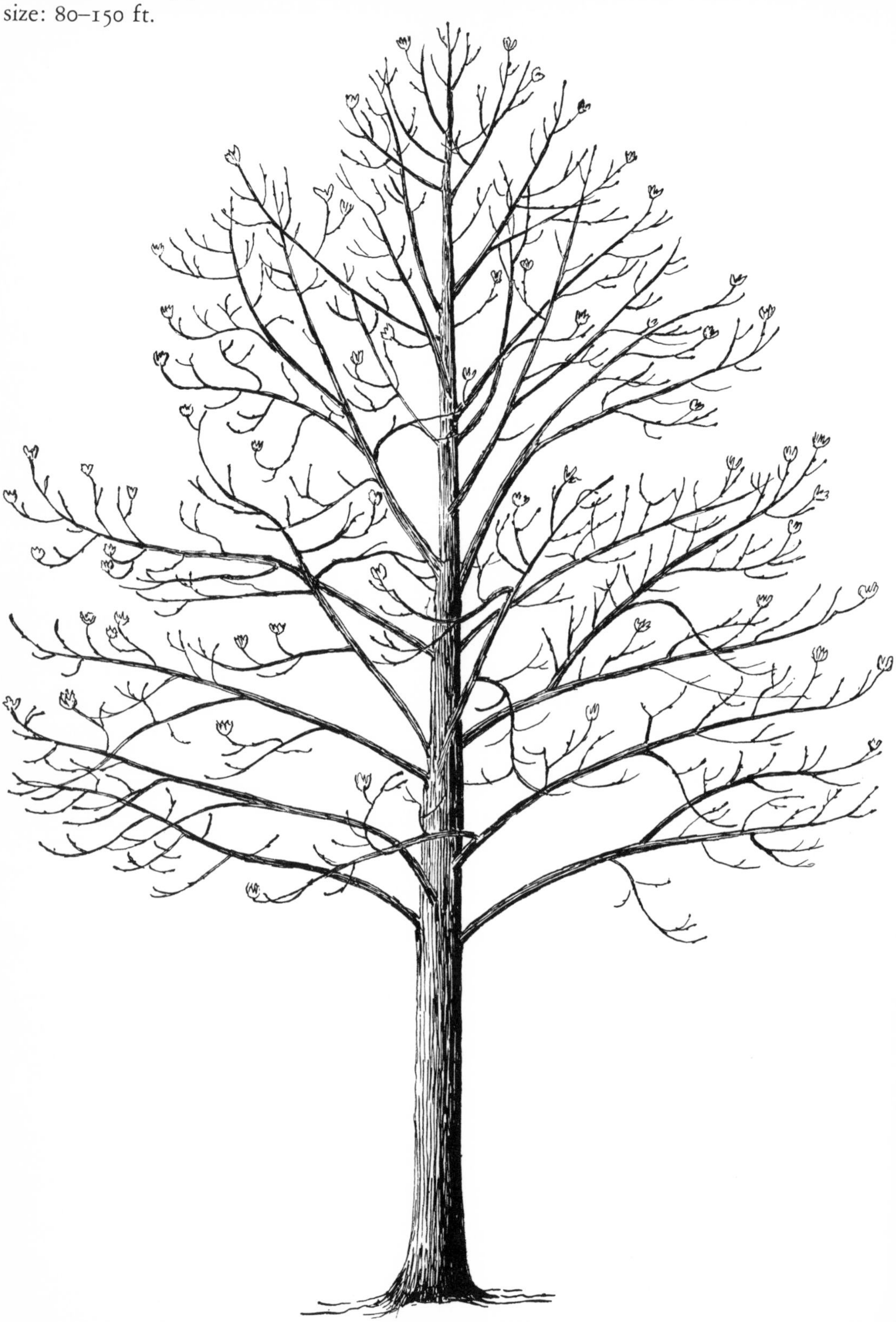

TULIP TREE
Liriodendron tulipifera

Because of the extraordinary beauty of its form, foliage, and flowers the Tulip Tree is often planted as a shade tree. Large specimens still stand in front of old colonial houses from Massachusetts south to Florida.

The trunk of the Tulip Tree grows straight and tall. The lower branches curve up slightly, while the upper branches grow at a steeper angle, so that the tree has a stately, symmetrical, oval crown. In winter, graceful curving twigs hold erect conelike seedpods. Later in the season when the seeds are gone, the remainder of the seedpod looks like a small, dry, tan, paper cup or miniature tulip, which makes it easy to identify this tree in the winter. It is the blossoms, however, that give the Tulip Tree its name. They are large, yellow-green flowers with orange blotches at the base, appearing in early summer.

This tree grows taller and is more massive than other deciduous trees, although its over-all proportions are not as heavy as those of the Sycamore. It is at its best on a wide, open lawn, where it will have plenty of room to develop in a dignified way.

The light, ash-gray bark on young Tulip Trees has shallow, whitish furrows, As the bark thickens on older trees, the furrows deepen into interlacing narrow ridges.

The Tulip Tree belongs to the Magnolia family, but it is often called the Yellow Poplar because of its soft wood. In Virginia and Pennsylvania, Indians called it Canoe Tree, because they made dugouts from the trunks.

SWEET GUM
Liquidambar styraciflua
size: 80–100 ft.

The Sweet Gum is one of the most beautiful trees of the southeastern part of the United States. This tree has a central, tapering trunk and slender side branches. The shape is rounded pyramidal. The details of the twigs and seedballs are rough and distinctive, but the whole effect of the tree is handsome at any time of year.

The Sweet Gum is easy to recognize in winter by the seedballs that hang all over the tree on slender stems. They are spiky, brown clusters of seed capsules about one and one-half inches in diameter. Another characteristic that shows up in winter is the variety of the bark on mature trees. The older twigs have corky ridges on the sides like wings, while the branches have a broken, warty bark. In some places the tree is called Alligator Bark because of this trait. In contrast, the soft, gray bark of the main trunk has deep furrows.

Its compact shape makes the Sweet Gum an ideal street tree. The interesting twigs and fruit are decorative in winter where it is used in a planting alongside of large buildings, and it is superb as an ornamental shade tree. Rich fall coloring is another asset.

Gums like rich, moist soil. Under ideal conditions they grow 80 to 100 feet tall. They will tolerate dry conditions but will not grow as large. Very few pests bother the Sweet Gum. It transplants easily and grows fairly rapidly. Sweet Gums are hardy from southern Connecticut, through the Ohio River valley, to Missouri and south.

BALD CYPRESS
Taxodium distichum
size: 60–120 ft.

BALD CYPRESS
Taxodium distichum

The shape of a Bald Cypress resembles a Spruce or Fir in its narrow, pyramidal form. The trunk is straight and tapering. When it becomes an old tree, and that could be hundreds of years old, the upper branches spread to make a broad, irregular head.

In winter, after the Cypress has lost its fine, needlelike leaves, the clusters of male flowers hang like tassels from the branches, swaying in the wind. The female flowers on the same tree develop into round, purplish cones about an inch in diameter. The reddish brown bark peels off in long narrow strips.

Bald Cypress is a native tree found along the coast in swamps from Delaware to Texas and up the Mississippi river and its tributaries as far north as Illinois. Where the roots are submerged part of the year, the trunk develops buttresses, and the roots form elongated cones called *knees*. These help anchor the tree. Despite the fact that it has shallow roots, this tree is rarely bothered by wind. If it grows on an average lawn, it will not have knees.

The distinctive narrow form of the Bald Cypress provides a sharp contrast with the average round-tree forms. Use this tree as a formal accent where Spruce will not grow. For all its size, the slender branches and fine twigs give it a texture that is pleasing as a contrast to Magnolia or Holly. As the tree matures, the broadening lower branches die back so that it is possible to walk under them. It is an interesting ornamental tree, but not a shade tree.

AMERICAN SYCAMORE
Platanus occidentalis
size: 70–140 ft.

This is a handsome giant of a tree. It may not be the tallest growing tree, but it has the most massive over-all proportions of any deciduous tree growing in the United States. In the open, magnificent specimens have been found 140 feet tall, with wide spreading limbs 100 feet across.

In the winter landscape, it is the bark that stands out most of all. Beginning on the lower part of the main trunk, the bark is a soft, smooth brown with patches of greenish and yellow inner bark showing where the outer bark has peeled off. The upper branches are bone white. These light-colored branches are striking against a blue winter sky. Many times in the woodland, the course of a stream is marked by the white Sycamore branches along the way. The bark of the European Sycamore (*Platanus acerifolia*) is not as white as the American variety.

Notice the multitudes of brown seedballs hanging on slender threads from the twigs, particularly at the top of the tree. It is often called Button Ball Tree. Another unique trait which shows up in winter is the way in which the secondary branches grow perpendicularly to the wide-spreading main branches.

Sycamores are as common as Elms from southern Maine through Iowa south to the Gulf. The European variety is often used as a street tree where there is room. The branches on all Sycamores start well up on the trunk, and other plants and lawns do well under them. They withstand smoke, soot, and dust and make fine fast-growing shade trees.

TULIP TREE

SWEET GUM

BALD CYPRESS

AMERICAN SYCAMORE

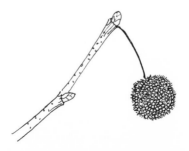

The dark red terminal buds of the Tulip Tree are egg-shaped. They are quite prominent, but the side buds are small and indistinct. The light gray twigs have complete encircling lines where scars are left by fallen leaves. On some twigs there will be light tan, papery, cup-shaped, empty seedpods.

The year-old twigs of the Sweet Gum acquire corky, winglike growths. The buds are large and shiny with many scales. The fruit is a round, tight cluster of seed capsules.

The small, immature twigs of the Bald Cypress drop off in winter. The older twigs or branchlets are reddish brown with small, round, green buds. Tassels of male flowers hang in clusters 3 to 6 inches long.

The Sycamore has slightly zigzag twigs which are moderately thick. The new twigs are green at first, then turn brown. The cone-shaped buds have a single scale. The fruit is a brown ball about an inch in diameter, composed of hairy seeds.

Since the Coffee Tree is bare six months of the year, it is easy to become acquainted with its winter form. The botanical name *Gymnocladus* means *naked branch*. In parts of Canada it is called Chicot—dead tree, and the southern mountaineers called it Stump Tree. Despite these unflattering names, it makes a striking, ornamental shade tree that would give interest and variety to any planting.

The Coffee Tree has large, upright, ascending limbs and thick, crooked branches and twigs. It has flowers on separate male and female trees. The female Coffee Tree has the largest pods of any pod-bearing tree. The brown pods are 6 to 10 inches long and 2 inches wide and hang, dry and rattling, in clusters all winter long. The early settlers tried to make coffee from the beans, hence the name Coffee Tree, although the coffee was not a success.

Even without the curious pods, this tree is dramatic. Its homely, rugged form would be handsome against the wall of a building or silhouetted against the sky, where the heavy twigs make a bold pattern.

Coffee Trees are medium-sized, about 40 to 70 feet tall with an oval crown. They are hardy from western New York and lower Ontario to Louisiana. This tree likes moist places, but will grow on hillsides. Since they have deep roots, plant them when young.

NORTHERN CATALPA
Catalpa speciosa
size: 25–50 ft.

NORTHERN CATALPA
Catalpa speciosa

This is one tree no one could possibly mistake in winter. The 10-to-18-inch-long, slender seedpods hang like hair all over the tree. The form of the tree itself is irregular and picturesque. In the open, the trunk may be short with thick, spreading, twisted limbs and a broad crown, while in the woods the tree may be tall, with a tapering trunk and branches that start high on the tree. The Catalpa has brittle branches, often injured by wind or ice, but any damage just seems to add to the ragged, homely look. The silhouette of a Catalpa tree in winter adds variety to any planting.

The Catalpa is very easy to plant and grows rapidly. It was used more frequently as an ornamental tree years ago for its showy white flowers. Large trees are often found in parks and cemeteries. It should be used more today where quick shade is needed. It will stand poor soil, drought, or salt air.

There is a dwarf, umbrella-shaped variety, *Catalpa bungei,* which was once very popular as an ornamental tree. It was pruned back to a ball each year. This form of tree could be used with great effect in a formal design. There is also a Japanese species with yellow flowers and a hybrid between the Eastern Catalpa (*Catalpa catalpa*) and the Japanese which has white flowers.

Catalpa speciosa originated in the Mississippi Valley. It is very hardy and has been planted all over the United States. Insects and pests do not bother it.

EASTERN REDBUD
Cercis canadensis

The Redbud is a very beautiful, small flowering tree. It has a flattish, curved top and branches that zigzag. Identifying it in winter is easy because of the short, brown pods hanging in close rows along the branches. There are no seedpods on the new growth at the ends of the branches. Sometimes the Redbud has one trunk, sometimes multiple trunks, and at other times the trunk divides near the base into several main branches, making a wide, spreading top. It is usually a small tree growing in the shade of larger trees and can grow as high as 30 to 40 feet.

The variety in the growth pattern of the Redbud makes this tree very useful in landscaping. It is lovely on the edge of a woodland or in a border of flowering shrubs. The winter silhouette casts interesting shadows. It is a good screening tree in winter because of its many twigs and seedpods and fits in well with contemporary architecture.

The Redbud grows quickly from seed. Although it has deep roots, it is easy to transplant. This tree is hardy from Connecticut west to Nebraska and south to Texas and northern Florida.

BLACK LOCUST
Robinia pseudoacacia

The Black Locust is also known as the Common Locust
or Acacia. The word *acacia* means thorny. There are pairs
of spines at each bud but, fortunately, there is a
thornless variety.

This is one of the pod-bearing trees. In winter, many
clusters of small, flat seedpods can be seen hanging on
the small branches. The silhouette of the Black Locust
against the sky is very artistic. Notice in the mature Locust
the comparative delicacy of the zigzag twigs to the stubby
branches, which makes the tree appear tough and fragile
at the same time. The branches are more or less horizontal.
The oblong crown is open and irregular. The bark also
looks tough and is brown with a reddish cast. Heavy
furrows form interlacing vertical ridges.

Because of its tall, fairly narrow shape and its height of
40 to 70 feet, this Locust accommodates itself well
to the average lawn. Several trees planted 12 to 15 feet
apart would give a pleasant, light shade. The branches
are too light to make a good screen or pattern in winter.
Black Locust trees grow very fast in deep, well-drained soil,
but they will tolerate poor soil and city smoke. This tree
is seriously attacked by the Locust borer, which can be
controlled by cutting off injured branches before June.
New branches will soon grow out and fill in the gap.

These Locusts grew originally in the Appalachian
Mountains but now are found in practically every state.
They have a tendency to sprout from the roots.

TWIG DETAILS

KENTUCKY COFFEE TREE

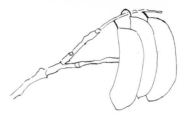

NORTHERN CATALPA

EASTERN REDBUD

BLACK LOCUST

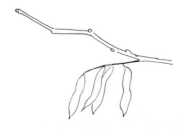

The mottled, gray-brown twig of the Coffee Tree is stout and crooked. The leaf buds are small and are hidden in the bark or notches of the scars made by the fallen leaves. It seems incredible that the 1-to-3-foot, doubly compound leaves could evolve from such a tiny bud. The seedpods are 6 to 10 inches long and 2 inches wide. The pods are brown.

The numerous seedpods that hang on the ends of the twigs of the Catalpa tree are 10 to 18 inches long. These brown pods split in late winter to release many flat, winged seeds. The twigs are smooth with embedded buds and conspicuous oval leaf scars. The end bud is missing.

The slender, dark-brown branches and twigs of the Redbud are literally hung with rows of small seedpods all winter. The pods are 2 to 3 inches long and are straight on the side where the stem joins the branch. The small, oval buds are pressed flat against the twigs.

In comparison to other pod-bearing trees, the Black Locust has delicate pods. They are thin and pale brown. The twigs are zigzag and may have spines on either side of inconspicuous buds.

GOLDENRAIN TREE
Koelrueteria paniculata
size: 20–30 ft.

GOLDENRAIN TREE
Koelrueteria paniculata

The Goldenrain Tree was brought to the United States long ago. It is also called the Varnish Tree or China Tree, since it came from China.

In winter, it has unique clusters of papery, lanternlike, brown seedpods at the tops of the branches. These evolve from conspicuous bright yellow flowers in late spring. The seedpods stay on the tree all winter despite their fragile appearance. The Goldenrain Tree has an irregular, artistic way of growing, with an open, loose crown. The orange-brown bark is broken up by flat, gray ridges in blocks. The whole tree has an exotic look in winter. Snow lying on the seedpods makes it look even more oriental. Its maximum height is about 30 feet. There is a columnar variety, *Koelrueteria paniculata* var. *fastigiata.*

Here is a small to medium-sized tree that will make a point of interest in any garden picture at any time of year. A Goldenrain Tree would always be interesting outside a picture window. It's a good choice for the corner of a house or a patio. A row of them would make a partial screen or divider. The Goldenrain Tree does not provide much shade. It is hardy from New York south and will tolerate either dry or wet soil.

SILK TREE
Albizzia julibrissin
size: 20–30 ft.

SILK TREE
Albizzia julibrissin

In winter, the shape of the Silk Tree, often called Mimosa, is quite distinctive with its several wide, spreading branches and its flat crown. No other tree has such a flat top. This tree grows sometimes with a single trunk and at other times with multiple trunks or very low branches. The pattern of the few thick branches and twigs is clean-looking in winter. It grows about 20 feet high and as wide. The Silk Tree also has conspicuous seedpods in winter which are light tan and very papery. They hang on the tree most of the winter in rustling clusters. The smooth, grayish tan bark does not have much interest.

The Silk Tree came originally from Persia. It is also called Powder-Puff Tree, on account of the fluffy, pink summer blossoms. This is the hardiest of the tropical trees. It is widely cultivated as far north as Massachusetts, although it may freeze back to the roots and come up anew each spring in the northern part of its range. Because of its very fast growth and umbrella shape, the Silk Tree is a good choice for a shade tree in some parts of the country. Several in a group give the impression of a long-established planting. Give Silk Trees a sunny spot and they will thrive. In some parts of the south, Silk Trees are subject to a fungus that wilts and kills the trees, but nurserymen are working on wilt-resistant strains in those areas and can advise.

SILK TREE

At the ends of the twigs on the Goldenrain Tree large clusters of brown, papery, three-sided seedpods hang on all winter. The individual pods are about one and one-half inches long and look like miniature Japanese lanterns. A round, black seed is attached to each rib of the pod. The twigs are grayish tan, with raised reddish lenticels or breathing pores and fat, pointed buds.

Small, inconspicuous, blunt buds grow along the Silk Tree's twigs. The end buds do not develop. The long, flat, tan, papery seedpods persist most of the winter in clusters at the ends of the tan twigs.

OSAGE ORANGE
Maclura pomifera
size: 30–50 ft.

OSAGE ORANGE
Maclura pomifera

The Osage Orange tree is ruggedly artistic. Its most noticeable characteristic in winter is the way in which its irregular branches grow in a series of curves or scallops. It has been called Bowwood or Bois d'arc because its wood made fine archery bows, but the name is singularly appropriate to the bows formed by the branches. The tree has stout branches starting low on the trunk and a ragged, broken crown.

The Osage Orange should be used more as a shade or ornamental tree for the unusual pattern of its branches in the winter. It makes a piece of growing sculpture for the garden. It is usually a small tree but can reach a height of 50 feet. A male tree should be planted because the large, greenish, orange-shaped fruit of the female tree litters the ground in the fall.

Planted close together as a hedge, the dense, thorny branches and the short trunks make an impenetrable barrier. In the country, it is often called Hedge Apple. Osage Orange is strong, hardy, and easy to propagate, as well as drought resistant. It grows in most of the United States, but it originated in Osage Indian territory in Arkansas, Oklahoma, and Texas.

The bark of the Osage Orange shows an orange color under the rough, shredded ridges of the brown outer layer.

COMMON PERSIMMON
Diosperos virginiana
size: 30–50 ft.

COMMON PERSIMMON
Diosperos virginiana

The crooked branches of the Persimmon tree and its round, irregular crown distinguish it from other trees in winter. In dry places where the soil is poor, it may be a small tree growing in thickets, but in a good location the Persimmon will grow as high as 50 feet. It has a short, slender trunk and slim branches that give it a fine texture from a distance.

After the leaves have fallen, the round, wrinkled fruit can be seen hanging all over the tree. Only the female Persimmon has fruit. This is among the few trees that has male and female flowers on separate trees. The fruits are about an inch and a half in diameter. The word *Diosperos* in the botantical name means *food for the gods,* but this is true only when the fruit is completely ripe. It is delicious to eat when, after a frost, it is ripe enough to fall off the tree.

The bark of this tree is quite distinctive and helps with the winter identification. It is a dark blackish brown and deeply cut into small, thick blocks. On young trees, orange color shows between the blocks.

Although the Persimmon is not a tree that is generally planted as an ornamental tree in the landscape, horticultural varieties are planted for their fruit. Their artistic branching patterns make them appealing as a lawn tree.

The Persimmon grows naturally in all the states in the eastern part of the country from Connecticut south and west to Iowa. There are only two species in the United States. The other grows in southwestern Texas.

BLACK WALNUT
Juglans nigra

The Black Walnut shows up against the winter landscape with a bare, gaunt look because of its sparse, heavy twigs and almost black color. The leaves fall early and appear late in the spring, so it is easy to spot among the other trees. The straight, massive trunk divides into rugged branches. The lower ones are horizontal while the upper ones ascend at a steep angle to form a sturdy, round head. The lowest branches die back early so that the tree has a high crown.

The Black Walnut has a wholesome, competent look. It is not often planted as a shade tree, but if one is found on a site, it should be encouraged, because it makes a magnificent specimen. Many times these trees are found growing along old fences or hedgerows where the squirrels have planted the nuts. Black Walnuts do not make good screens, however. Their twigs are not dense, and the tree is bare too much of the year. Plant one in the center of the lawn where it will have room to spread.

The bark is almost black and is deeply grooved and broken up into diamond-shaped furrows.

This is a fast-growing, hardwood tree. Twenty years after a nut has been planted, a tree will have grown about 30 feet tall, and trees 100 feet tall are fairly common. Walnuts require neutral, well-drained soil and full sun. They are found from southern Ontario to western Texas. Their one fault is that many plants, especially Pines, Crabapples, and Viburnums will not grow near them. Something in the roots seems to poison the soil as far as those plants are concerned.

SHAGBARK HICKORY
Carya ovata
size: 80–100 ft.

SHAGBARK HICKORY
Carya ovata

The Shagbark Hickory is a ragged, casual-looking tree. The form is tall and slender with an irregular, round-topped crown. In the forest the trunk is often straight and clear for 50 feet or more, although sometimes it divides. These trees grow eventually to a height of 80 to 100 feet. The curving twigs are stout in comparison with the slender branches. The twigs have beautifully pointed, egg-shaped end buds about an inch long which help to identify the tree in winter.

It is the gray bark that is most unique and gives the tree its name. Long, shaggy strips are attached by their centers leaving each end free to curl. On young trees the bark is smooth.

As an ornamental tree, the Shagbark gives an air of country informality and spacious room to a house and garden. A group of these trees on a lawn is a pleasing sight. Because of their height, they would make good background trees with smaller trees planted in front.

Hickories like deep, fertile soil. Growing wild, they indicate good farm land. Their natural range covers the eastern part of the United States west to the plains. They do not grow along the Southern coastline nor around the Gulf.

The Shellbark Hickory (*Carya laciniosa*) is a very similar species, also with shaggy bark. The end buds are blunt, and the twigs are light brown.

TWIG DETAILS

OSAGE ORANGE

COMMON PERSIMMON

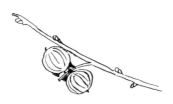

BLACK WALNUT

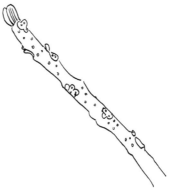

SHAGBARK HICKORY

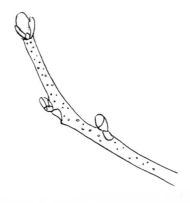

At each scar left by a fallen leaf, there is a sturdy, short, straight spine. The orange-brown twigs zigzag slightly. The ball-shaped buds are hardly noticeable, and the end buds are false and do not develop.

The hairy twigs of the Persimmon are slender and brown, eventually becoming gray. The buds are small and are covered with two very dark-brown scales. The buds at the ends of the twigs are false and do not develop.

The sparse, stout, brown twigs of the Black Walnut are covered with rust-colored hairs. The buds at the ends of the twigs are large, gray, and fuzzy. The fuzzy side buds are smaller and round. The scars left by the fallen leaves are heart-shaped.

The beautiful end buds of the Shagbark Hickory are one half to three quarters of an inch long. They are egg-shaped with downy, overlapping scales. The outer scales are dark and narrow; the inner scales are light colored and velvety. The twigs are reddish brown with heart-shaped leaf scars.

WESTERN SOAPBERRY
Sapindus drummondi

This little-known tree is a native of the Western plains. It is often called Wild China Tree because of the resemblance of its fruit to that of the Chinaberry (*Melia azedarach*), which was imported into this country many years ago and widely planted in the South. Clusters of translucent, yellow berries at the ends of the twigs make it easy to identify the Soapberry in the winter. They are about the same size as cranberries, and, when the winter sun shines through them, the berries are a cheerful sight, but they are reported to be poisonous. The Indians crushed them with water to make a lather for soap, hence the name.

The Soapberry is tall with a rounded head. It has a few large, irregular branches with many short, twisted twigs. The branches start high, so it makes a good lawn tree. It is a small to medium-sized tree, growing from 25 to 40 feet tall.

The bark is reddish brown, broken into long, narrow scales. The Soapberry does well in hot, dry locations. It is hardy from Missouri to southern Colorado and south through Texas and Arizona. It will grow readily from seed.

JAPANESE PAGODA TREE
Sophora japonica

This tree is also known as the Chinese Scholar Tree and was originally a native of China and Korea. Along its way around the world, the Arabian name *Sophora,* which means *tree with pea-shaped blossoms,* was added. It was very popular in Victorian gardens but has been forgotten until recently.

In winter, it is easily distinguished by its unusual seedpods and green twigs. The seedpods look like beads on a string. They are a light yellowish tan color in the winter and seem to envelop the tree in a golden haze.

The spreading shape of the mature tree somewhat resembles the Elm, although it is not such a large tree. In the North, it will grow 25 feet tall; in the South it becomes larger. The spreading, upright branches are irregular. This spreading shape alone would make it a valuable addition to our list of garden trees, but it is a beautiful and unusual specimen all through the year. It is an excellent shade tree for a patio or a picture window. The bark is grayish brown and not outstanding.

City conditions do not bother this tree. It is strong and vigorous and not troubled by disease. Transplanting is easily done, and average soil and growing conditions suit it. There is a weeping form, *Sophora japonica* var. *pendula,* and a pyramidal form, *Sophora japonica* var. *pyramidalis.*

WESTERN SOAPBERRY

JAPANESE PAGODA TREE

The slightly angled twigs of the Soapberry are greenish when they are young but turn pale gray as the tree matures. There are numerous lenticels, or breathing pores. In contrast to the gray twigs, the buds are brown, round, and fuzzy. The yellow, translucent berries hang on the tree most of the winter.

The twigs of the Japanese Pagoda Tree are green when they are new. They are smooth with small, fuzzy, brown buds almost hidden by the triangular scars left by the fallen leaves. At the tips of the twigs are sprays of yellow-gold seedpods. There are from one to six seeds in the pods.

SAUCER MAGNOLIA
Magnolia soulangeana

This is a hybrid form of a magnolia that grows wild in China and Japan. It is the showiest of all the magnolias and is generally planted for its spectacular, rose-colored spring flowers. It is a handsome tree in the winter too. The sturdy, silvery gray branches and twigs make a beautiful silhouette. It may grow 20 to 25 feet high with a rounded crown. The trunk usually divides into several ascending branches or into multiple trunks. The twigs curve up, and on the ends are large, furry, greenish buds that add to the winter beauty of the tree and make it easy to identify. The bark is a smooth silver-gray with a few horizontal, darker gray markings.

The multiple-branching habit of the Saucer Magnolia makes it useful in landscaping where vertical lines need to be softened. It is handsome in plantings around public buildings or as an accent at the focal point of a planting design. The pale gray bark contrasts nicely with evergreens or a dark-colored house. It is one tree that is beautiful every month of the year.

This Magnolia is hardy as far north as Boston, Massachusetts, but north of Washington, D.C., the early spring flowers may be blighted by frost. It stands city conditions well.

CUCUMBER TREE
Magnolia acuminata

The Cucumber Tree is a perfect oval. Notice how the lower branches droop and then turn up, almost sweeping the ground when the tree is grown in the open. The higher the branches, the more steeply they turn upward from the straight central trunk, which makes a beautifully symmetrical tree. The glossy, stout twigs have large terminal buds that are covered with greenish, silky fur.

This member of the Magnolia family differs from the others in several ways. It is the only one with rough bark, gray-brown with narrow flaky ridges and long vertical grooves. It is the hardiest of the native Magnolias, growing wild from Lake Ontario south through Alabama and central Mississippi, west to Arkansas. It is also the largest, rapidly attaining a height of 50 to 80 feet.

The winter silhouette is handsome. The Cucumber Tree makes a very ornamental tree for formal planting along an avenue or as a shade tree on a lawn. It is hard to transplant because of its brittle roots, but it grows easily from seed.

FRINGE TREE
Chionanthus virginica
size: 15–25 ft.

FRINGE TREE
Chionanthus virginica

Among the loveliest and most striking of native flowering trees is the Fringe Tree. It is also called Old-Man's-Beard and Snow Flower. The illustration shows what an interesting pattern the tortuous, spreading branches make in winter. The Fringe Tree usually resembles a shrub, sending up several stout branches that curl in every direction to make a wide-spreading crown. It can be trained to a single stem if desired and, under those conditions, will make a small tree 15 to 25 feet tall. The branches and twigs are coarse enough to show up well against a building or mass of evergreens and make a distinctive pattern and decorative design. The bark is brownish red and scaly.

Use this charming little tree in foundation plantings where height and interest are needed, perhaps at the corner of a house or against a blank wall. Its coarse texture and irregular habit of growth make it useful in informal plantings.

The Fringe Tree is native wherever there is rich, moist soil, from New Jersey south to central Florida and west to Oklahoma and Texas.

WEEPING CHERRY
Prunus subhirtella var. *pendula*
size: 20–40 ft.

WEEPING CHERRY
Prunus subhirtella var.
pendula

Flowering Cherries are usually associated with Japan because of the beautiful Cherry trees along the tidal basin in Washington, D.C. The Weeping Cherry comes from Japan also.

The sturdy, straight trunk of the Cherry divides into large branches, which grow at artistic angles. The contrastingly delicate outer branches flow out and up to fall over from a broad, irregular crown, creating a weeping effect. Along the lower parts of the branches are innumerable short, curving twigs. The whole effect of the tree is artistic, a contrast in stiffness and grace. The outline of the tree is just as beautiful in winter when the bare branches show up as it is when the branches are covered with a cloud of pink blossoms.

The bark is a warm gray with elongated lenticels, or breathing pores, that are golden brown and horizontal. As the tree matures, the bark roughens and becomes scaly.

The Weeping Cherry makes a lovely single ornamental specimen plant where interest can be concentrated on its unusual branches. It makes a good background for a piece of statuary and fits in perfectly in an oriental setting or with evergreens. Of course, the Cherries are very hardy.

TWIG DETAILS

SAUCER MAGNOLIA

CUCUMBER TREE

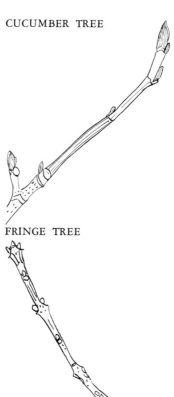

FRINGE TREE

WEEPING CHERRY

Against the silver-gray of the Saucer Magnolia twigs, the large, furry end buds present a pleasing greenish gray. The side buds are smaller. The scars made by the fallen leaves are crescent-shaped.

The velvety, blunt-pointed end buds of the Cucumber Tree are pale green and are three quarters of an inch long. The side buds are smaller. The twigs are a smooth, reddish brown becoming greenish towards the ends. The leaf scars are narrow crescents.

The moderately stout, slightly angled twigs on the Fringe Tree have oval, pointed buds about one eighth of an inch long. The twigs are light orange-brown and slightly downy.

The twigs of the Weeping Cherry have two end buds, with another just below. The small, pointed buds are reddish brown and lie flat against the pale tan twigs. The twigs are streaked with red and have reddish breathing pores.

WHITE OR PAPER BIRCH
Betula papyrifera

The white bark of the Paper Birch makes instant identification easy at any time of year. It is one of the favorite trees in the northern section of the country, where it grows along the roadsides and rocky shores of lake and ocean.

This is a dainty tree, the queen of the forest. It grows sometimes in a single trunk and sometimes in a clump. The branches are slender, and the twigs are fine and flexible. This gives the tree a lacy effect in winter. The crown is irregular and, as the tree becomes older, may become open. This Birch is usually considered a small tree, but it can grow 80 feet tall. It has a gaiety and grace no other tree can equal. It is beautiful on a lawn mixed with evergreens where its white bark shows up against the deep green, and the light green foliage adds life to the stiffer conifers.

A clump of Birch looks well at the corner of a house or on a patio. A circle or line of these trees would make a good division between one part of the garden and another or a decorative *allée*. It does not have a large enough spread to make a good shade tree. There is also a weeping variety that is very popular for ornamental planting.

The white bark has a chalky look. It peels off in paper-thin, horizontal layers. Stories of how the Indians used birch bark for utensils and canoes are told in all school books. As the tree becomes old, the outer bark rolls back and curls showing black patches. During the winter, small seed cones an inch or more long can be seen hanging on the outer twigs.

Birches should be planted in early spring. There is a bronze Birch borer that bothers Birches and causes the tops to die. If the infested part of the tree is cut back to the ground, a new tree will soon grow from the stump. South of New York State, the European variety (*Betula alba*) is more reliable.

GRAY BIRCH
Betula populifolia
size: 20–30 ft.

GRAY BIRCH
Betula populifolia

Careful observation is needed to tell the Gray Birch from a young Paper Birch in the winter since they both have white bark. To help in identifying it, look for the strong and numerous V-shaped, dark marks at the base of the branches. It also has the dark, horizontal markings lower on the trunk which all Birches have. The dull, chalky-white bark does not peel off easily. This is a smaller tree than the Paper Birch. The slender trunks, which generally grown in clumps, are rarely more than 20 to 30 feet tall. The crown is long, narrow, and open. The branches, which start high on the trunks, are short and slender and sometimes droop. The twigs are fine and wiry.

The slender form and relatively small size of the Gray Birch make it useful in landscaping where a tree of limited size is needed. It will not grow out of proportion if it is planted at the corner of a house with some low evergreens. The lacy texture of the fine branches is restful in a small garden. Birches seem at their best in natural plantings. Their narrow shape makes an interesting avenue of trees with the trunks resembling white columns.

In the northern part of the United States where this Birch grows naturally, it is often found bent over from the weight of snow and ice. It will grow as far south as West Virginia and Ohio. Gray Birch will grow in poor soil, but it prefers sunshine and a well-drained spot.

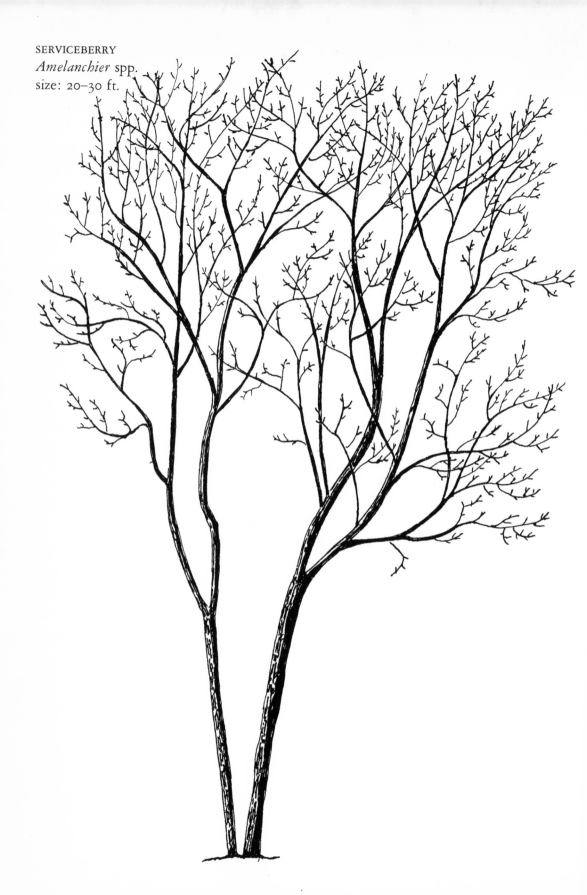

SERVICEBERRY
Amelanchier spp.

This is a dainty native tree. It was discovered early by settlers and brought under cultivation. George Washington planted some near the entrance columns of Mount Vernon. It is also called Sarvistree or Shadbush, since the flowers bloom when the Shad are running in the tidal rivers.

The Serviceberry may have one trunk or several. The slender branches reach up, and the twigs are fine. The whole effect of the tree in winter is delicate, and yet the wood is strong and resists breaking under snow and ice. In winter, the bark of the Serviceberry is outstanding. It is satin smooth, light gray with a pinkish cast, and striped, brightening the dull colors of the winter scene.

The Serviceberry has many uses in landscaping. It is a small tree reaching an ultimate height of only 20 to 30 feet, so it stays in scale with small homes. It also looks well at the entrance of a large building. Along the edge of a woodland, by a pool, or as a high accent in a shrubbery border, the Serviceberry is in its element. A row of these trees is lovely, and the multiple trunks make a good screen.

Serviceberry is very hardy, thriving on poor soil. It grows naturally from the northern border of the United States south to Florida and west as far as the Dakotas.

RUSSIAN OLIVE
Eleagnus angustifolia
size: 15–20 ft.

RUSSIAN OLIVE
Eleagnus angustifolia

The Russian Olive was originally brought to this country from Europe and central Asia. It is cultivated primarily for its silvery foliage and is a small tree about 15 to 20 feet high at maturity, with an irregular, rounded crown. The branches curve in an artistic way. Its many fine twigs give it a delicate look. The whole tree is so dainty in a ragged way that the mass fades out in winter, and it should not be used in landscaping where a strong, year-round screen is needed. Despite the light look of the whole tree, the dark charcoal-gray bark shows up well against the more neutral tones of other plants.

This little tree is nice in a border planting or in a group where its fine texture contrasts with other plants. Planted in a large tub, it has an oriental look.

The Russian Olive is very hardy. It grows from Maine south through the great plains, where it is especially planted for its drought-resistant qualities. City smoke and dust do not bother it, and it takes to the seashore and salt air with aplomb.

TWIG DETAILS

PAPER BIRCH

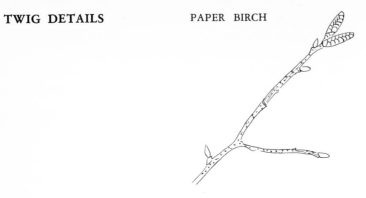

GRAY BIRCH

SERVICEBERRY

RUSSIAN OLIVE

132

Notice the two or three male catkins at the end of the twigs; the female seed cones hang further back on the twigs. They are brown, cylindrical masses of seed strung on stalks. The twigs are reddish brown with noticeable lenticels. Sometimes the twigs are fuzzy on the under sides. The buds are pointed and slightly sticky to touch.

These are the finest twigs of any hardwood. They are tough and wiry, colored a dull gray or brown with a rough warty surface coated with grayish film. The small, pointed buds are smooth and slightly sticky to touch, and there is usually a solitary catkin at the end of the twig.

Reddish brown overlaid with a grayish film distinguishes the slender, somewhat zigzag twigs of the Serviceberry. The buds are slender and sharply pointed, like those of the Beech, with reddish brown scales sometimes tipped with black. The leaf scars are narrowly crescent-shaped.

This twig is easily identified by its fineness, its silvery scales, and the numerous, unbranched thorns.

This Birch grows further south than any of the other birches, from Massachusetts and Minnesota to the Gulf, particularly along the muddy banks of the Mississippi River and its tributaries. There it may attain a height of 80 to 90 feet, but it is more normally about 50 feet tall. A slender, graceful tree with a round irregular head, it is apt to grow in several trunks which lean away from each other. The branches, which start high on the trunk, are slender. The shiny chestnut-brown twigs have catkins at the tips.

The bark of the River Birch is its distinguishing characteristic. Young trees have silky, outward curling, papery scales with a metallic, cinnamon color and pinkish brown layers underneath. The bark is marked by narrow, longitudinal breathing pores. When the tree becomes old, the bark on the lower part of the trunk becomes deep reddish black with furrows. It is very beautiful.

The River Birch makes a desirable ornamental tree for the average-sized home, if there is a moist, well-drained, sunny spot. Use it on a patio or leaning over a pool. River Birch is a good choice for naturalistic planting, since it is shaggy and irregular. It grows quickly and makes a good screen or divider for a garden, will sprout quickly from seed, and also transplants easily.

This tree has quite a distinctive habit of growth. The crown is often flattened, open, and unsymmetrical. The twisted branches spread out in an angular fashion holding out many crooked smaller branches that also grow out at an angle. The mass of the tree seems to be divided into definite sections made up of each large branch and its twigs, rather than the over-all pattern of most trees. In winter, the shiny green twigs are noticeable.

On young trees, the greenish bark is cracked into tan-colored blocks. As the tree becomes older the bark turns reddish brown with twisted ridges washed with gray. The bark is aromatic.

In the northern limit of its range in southern Maine, it is a small tree. The further south it grows, down into northern Florida and eastern Texas, the larger the Sassafras becomes. In the Smoky Mountains, it may reach a height of 90 feet.

The Sassafras is an artistic looking tree, almost oriental in shape. It is useful in a wooded area or as a background tree and would make a unique shade tree. The Sassafras is the only tree that has three distinct shapes of leaves. One is mitten-shaped with a lobe on one side, one has three lobes, and the other has one lobe or is entire.

Sassafras will grow on stony or sandy soil as well as a fertile lawn. The tree is difficult to transplant but will grow quickly from seeds or root cuttings.

TWIG DETAILS

RIVER BIRCH

SASSAFRAS

The smooth, slender twigs of the River Birch are red-brown in color, with many pale breathing pores. The pointed, oval buds are slightly sticky. There are staminate, pollen-bearing catkins in clusters of two or three at the ends of the twigs.

The Sassafras twigs are a shining yellow-green color, with some brown tinges. They are often crooked. The scars left by the fallen leaves are half rounds. The terminal bud is larger than the side buds, usually about a half inch long. It has several yellow-green downy scales.

YELLOWWOOD
Cladrastis lutea
size: 30–50 ft.

YELLOWWOOD
Cladrastis lutea

The Yellowwood is a rare and beautiful tree native to the southeastern part of the United States. Notice in winter how the short trunk divides within several feet of the ground into a few, large, steeply ascending limbs with narrow crotches. These subdivide again, ending in slightly angled, horizontal branches and twigs. At the ends of the twigs, a few clusters of flattened 2-inch seedpods hang on the tree most of the winter, although the majority of them blow off early in the season.

The bark is thin and smooth, gray rather like that of the Beech, with bulges that resemble muscles. The heart wood is yellow, which gives the tree its name.

The Yellowwood is a perfect ornamental tree at any time of year. It is medium-sized, growing at most to a height of 50 feet. Pruning the lower branches when it is young gives it a high crown. Other plants do well underneath this tree because its roots go so deep. Its lovely spreading shape makes it a good shade tree for any place in the garden. In the spring, it has panicles of drooping white flowers like Wisteria. Give it a fertile, alkaline, well-drained soil, and it will quickly grow into a fine specimen.

SILVERBELL
Halesia monticola
size: 20–25 ft.

Charming and graceful describe the winter form of the Silverbell tree. As a young tree it has a pyramidal head, but as the tree matures and reaches a height of 20 to 25 feet, it develops a loose rounded head. The Silverbell usually has several trunks and wide-spreading, slender branches that end in graceful curves. Unique four-winged fruit follows the pendant, white spring flowers and hangs on late into the winter, so that the tree is easily identified. The fruit is about one and one half inches long, reddish brown in the fall, turning dry and corky at maturity.

The bark has reddish brown rectangular blocks with narrow, gray ridges. On the small branches, the bark is shreddy.

This is a delightful, informal tree. It is particularly lovely planted at the edge of a woodland or against a background of evergreens. The multiple trunks and spreading branches have a decorative pattern that is helpful in softening strong vertical lines on a building. Use it in a place where its low branches will not be disturbed, perhaps in a corner planting with spring bulbs underneath. It has enough twigs to make a fair screen in winter.

Silverbell is a native in the South from West Virginia to Texas. Give it a sheltered place, and it is hardy as far north as Massachusetts. The variety *Halesia carolina* is not considered as desirable as *Halesia monticola* because the flowers come out later and are almost hidden by the leaves.

BLACK GUM
Nyssa sylvatica
size: 60–80 ft.

BLACK GUM
Nyssa sylvatica

The Black Gum has a straight trunk and many slender branches distinguished by numerous small branchlets that reach up. This gives the tree a very striking effect in winter which many people think is artistic. The tree cannot easily be mistaken for any other tree, even by a novice. The Black Gum has a dense, pyramidal crown.

The bark is a dark reddish brown, almost black. It becomes an inch or more thick on old trees, and has deep furrows and irregular ridges breaking into square blocks. Planted as an ornamental tree on a lawn, it is usually a small tree. Where it grows wild in a wet or swampy place, it may grow to 60 or 80 feet.

In the South, the Black Gum is called Sour Gum. New Englanders use the Indian name Tupelo, and further west it is called Pepperidge. It has probably the most vivid scarlet fall coloring of any tree. Black Gum is hardy over the eastern part of the United States, barring most of Maine and Florida.

A low, moist place in the garden would be ideal for a Black Gum. It makes a strikingly unusual ornamental tree. It is hard to establish but easy to grow from seed. The roots are shallow, so it is weak in strong winds.

YELLOWWOOD

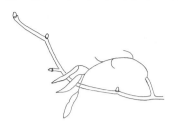

SILVERBELL

BLACK GUM

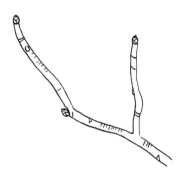

The slightly angular twigs of the Yellowwood are brittle. The scar left by the fallen leaf goes completely around the bud. The buds are pointed. Some of the dry, tan seedpods, which are about 2 inches long, hang on the twigs in clusters for part of the winter.

The slightly shreddy bark on the smaller branches of the Silverbell tree is also found on some of the twigs. The buds are reddish, sharply pointed, with four fleshy scales. Clusters of four-winged fruit hang on the year-old twigs part of the winter.

The terminal buds on the Black Gum twigs are fat and pointed. They are small and reddish brown with five visible scales. The lighter-colored twigs are smooth and slender. The scars left by the fallen leaves are semicircular.

AMERICAN MOUNTAIN ASH
Sorbus americana

The native Mountain Ash is a small tree. Sometimes it has several trunks, and other times a single trunk with steeply ascending branches that form a shapely oval crown. The whole appearance of the tree is neat and smooth. It grows about 20 feet tall but may reach as high as 30 feet under ideal conditions. The slim trunk has smooth, brown bark with green undertones, and the twigs are stout.

Clusters of showy, bright orange-red berries appear late in the fall. If there are no flocks of birds to devour them, they will hang on the tree part of the winter.

The European Mountain Ash (*Sorbus aucuparia*) is very similar. It is usually planted as an ornamental tree because it always has a single trunk and is easily accessible from the nurseries. There is a pyramidal form, *Sorbus fastigiata,* and a weeping variety, *Sorbus pendula.* This is a very useful tree for landscaping because of its prim, precise winter form. It always looks well groomed. It is a nice-sized tree for a small lawn. Mountain Ash would make a good screen or a symmetrical row of trees. Despite its prim appearance, it looks well in a natural, informal planting with evergreens or native shrubs, such as Viburnums. The Mountain Ash grows fairly rapidly. It is hardy in the northern part of the country from Manitoba and Maine down the mountain ranges to the Carolinas, wherever there is plenty of moisture.

In some parts of its range, Mountain Ash is bothered by borers. Where that is so, the nurserymen will know, and the Korean Mountain Ash, *Sorbus alnifolia,* is the one to plant.

JAPANESE MAPLE
Acer palmatum
size: 10–20 ft.

JAPANESE MAPLE
Acer palmatum

As its name suggests, this little Maple was imported from Japan. It has an oriental look and is very artistic in a restrained way. It has a short trunk that divides into several branches, curving up to make an irregular, rounded head. This Maple is a dwarf, bushy tree, rarely reaching 20 feet in height after many years of slow growth. The fine, opposite twigs are reddish, and in winter this trait gives the tree a warm color. The bark is light gray, with markings of darker gray.

Use this little gem where its beauty can be appreciated. It is fine, of course, in a Japanese-style garden or in a rock garden where its small scale enhances the miniature alpine flowers. Give it a background of evergreen or a white wall to show off its fine branches and the reddish color of the lacy leaves. Put one behind a translucent plastic screen and shine a light against it at night for a shadow pattern. One would fit in well in a large, sunny planter box. Give this little tree room to develop slowly where it will not be smothered by faster growing plants. The Japanese Maple is very hardy and it likes a sunny spot.

HOPA CRAB
Malus hopa

The Hopa Crab is one of the largest of the Oriental flowering Crabapples. It grows about 20 to 25 feet high. The trunk is short, dividing into many curving branches and making a rounded head. The secondary branches are stout, with numerous thick, spurlike twigs spaced at close intervals along them. In winter, the warm grayish brown bark seems to have a pinkish cast. The bark is smooth on young trees but becomes rougher and more scaly as the tree matures.

The Hopa Crab is a vigorous tree. It will grow wherever Apples are hardy, over a wide area of the United States. It is dependable under various trying conditions of soil and weather. Because of its dense habit of growth and low branches, it makes a good, tall screen. One would make a gorgeous ornamental tree on a lawn or as a feature in a garden design. The formal, clean, winter silhouette is decorative when used in large-scale plantings around schools, public buildings, and factories. It is especially lovely in the spring when it becomes a tremendous pink bouquet.

The native Crabapples are affected by Juniper rust, a fungus disease which makes disfiguring orange-brown spots on the leaves when they grow near Junipers. The Oriental Crabapples are not bothered by this disease.

SMOKE TREE
Cotinus obovatus
size: 6–25 ft.

SMOKE TREE
Cotinus obovatus

This is one of the rarest of American trees. It is closely related to the Sumac and originally was found in an area in the center of the country, through parts of Tennessee, Kentucky, Missouri, Arkansas, and Texas. It is the very similar European variety, *Cotinus coggygria,* that is often planted in gardens.

The Smoke Tree is a large bush or tree, anywhere from 6 to 25 feet tall but usually averaging about 15 feet in height. It has multiple trunks, and the branching habit is unusual and distinctive. The twigs grow in clusters like spokes at long intervals along the branches and at the ends of the branches. The young twigs are a warm purplish red. The very thin bark is light gray and is broken into furrows with oblong scales.

The winter pattern of the Smoke Tree is clean-cut and decorative. It is a neat tree. Because of the multiple trunks, the tree fills in well at the corner of a house or in a large shrubbery border. It provides a decided accent, and its unusual character would make it interesting in a modern design. The twigs are so sparse that the Smoke Tree does not make a good screen in winter.

The name Smoke Tree comes from the peculiar masses of cloudlike purple hairs borne at the ends of the branches in late summer. The Smoke Tree is hardy from Maine south to Alabama. City conditions do not affect it. It does well with average soil and moisture.

TWIG DETAILS

AMERICAN MOUNTAIN ASH

JAPANESE MAPLE

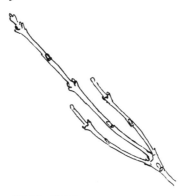

HOPA CRAB

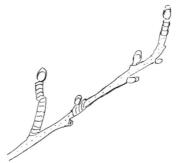

SMOKE TREE

The stout twigs of the Mountain Ash are gray-brown. They have large, pale breathing pores, or lenticels. The buds are dark red and gummy. The end buds are one half inch long, while the side buds are smaller and pressed against the twigs.

The small, slender twigs of the Japanese Maple are a shiny red. The fat, pointed little buds are brown.

Pink shines through the grayish tan secondary branches of the Hopa Crab. It has short spurlike twigs with fuzzy, green buds partly enclosed by pinkish scales.

The shiny purple twigs of the Smoke Tree are quite distinctive in the winter. They have small, pointed, black buds. The scars made by the fallen leaves are oval. The breathing pores are light colored.

FLOWERING DOGWOOD
Cornus florida

Wherever it grows in the eastern half of the United States, from Massachusetts to Florida, the native Flowering Dogwood reigns supreme as the best-loved flowering tree both in the wild and as a garden specimen. In the open, the shape of the Dogwood is spreading and well proportioned, while in the woods it often grows taller and more irregular. It is a small tree and seldom grows more than 30 feet tall.

Notice the spreading branches that grow in flat layers. This is a very distinctive trait. Each branch has many short twigs curving up like finger tips of an open hand. At the tip of many of these twigs, there is a small, turnip-shaped flower bud. When they open in the spring before the leaves come out, tiers of white or pink flowers cover the tree.

Dogwood bark is gray when the tree is small. Later on it turns reddish brown and breaks into square, blocky scales. The smooth, slender twigs are purple, covered with a gray, frosty bloom. These twigs add a warm color to the winter scene.

The winter form of the Dogwood is lacy. It is especially beautiful when it shows up in silhouette against a blank wall. This is a valuable tree for any size garden, a picture of beauty all year. The spreading, horizontal branches help to break up tall, vertical lines of buildings and are restful. The Flowering Dogwood is useful in large-scale plantings around public buildings or in parks. Along the edge of a woodland or in a natural planting, it is in its element but fits in equally well in a formal garden. Despite its dainty appearance, the Dogwood is a strong tree with a long life.

COCKSPUR HAWTHORN
Crataegus crus-galli
size: 15–20 ft.

HAWTHORN
Crataegus spp.

This is a large, complicated genus, as botanists describe it. The illustration shows the Cockspur, a common variety of Hawthorn. Generally Hawthorns are all distinguished by their very dense, twiggy habit of growth and their long thorns. The crowns vary from broad rounded to narrow rounded. The homely looking branches spread out with a characteristic zigzag, and the very numerous twigs are crooked also.

In England, the Hawthorns were used extensively for hedging. The name *haw* meant hedge. They are small trees and grow on an average of about 15 feet tall. The trunk is sometimes single and sometimes multiple. There is a columnar variety, *Crataegus monogyna stricta*. The bark is gray or reddish brown and very scaly.

The Hawthorns are rough-textured trees with a ragged look. They are grown for their picturesque traits, as well as the pink or white flowers and showy red or orange berries that hang on the tree well into the winter. The fruit is small and applelike. On some varieties, the fruit hangs in clusters. Washington Thorn, *Crataegus phaenopyrum,* is usually planted for its winter display of fruit.

Hawthorns are fine for camouflaging a view. They can be sheared into a high compact hedge, and a group of them is effective as an accent near a large building. A row of these trees is also striking. Not everyone likes the perfume of the flowers, so it would be just as well not to plant them too near a house or patio.

Hawthorns grow over a wide territory from Maine south. They will grow in poor soil and stand drought.

TEA CRAB
Malus hupehensis
size: 10–15 ft.

TEA CRAB
Malus hupehensis

Originally this Oriental Crabapple was grown for the leaves, which in China were made into tea. It has a very unique and interesting shape. The curving branches spread out from the short trunk into a wide, spreading fan. The branches are studded with short, spurlike twigs. The smooth bark is reddish brown.

One way to add character to a garden planting is to choose a tree with a decided pattern of growth. This Crab has one, and it is easy to espalier the fan shape against a wall. The Tea Crabs grow only 10 to 15 feet high, so they will not grow out of bounds. A pair trained into formal shapes on either side of a walk or driveway would be as dramatic as spread peacocks' tails. The effect of the widely spreading branches also resembles a fountain.

Like all Crabapples, the tree is hardy wherever Apples grow and it is beautiful all year.

SARGENT CRAB
Malus sargenti
size: 6–8 ft.

SARGENT CRAB
Malus sargenti

If any tree could be called square in shape, the Sargent Crab comes closest to it. The trunk is very short and sometimes multiple. The branches start close to the base, curving and spreading upward with many intertwining, horizontal branches. The smaller branches are lined with many short, spurlike twigs. In winter the smooth, shiny, reddish brown bark on the intertwining branches adds warmth to the prevailing neutral tones. Snow on the branches makes the color and pattern even more pleasing.

This is the smallest of the Oriental Crabapples. While the Americans worked for better fruit on Crabapples, the Chinese and Japanese tried for more flowers and more interesting forms. This tree grows only 6 to 8 feet tall. Its small scale is helpful in gardens where space is limited. Use it in foundation planting, in a group on a lawn, or in a border. It makes a decorative low screen, and would be beautiful planted around a patio where its loveliness could be enjoyed the year around. One would be charming in a large, square planter with some prostrate Junipers below it.

Sargent Crabs are hardy over a wide range from the Canadian border south, wherever Apples grow.

TWIG DETAILS

FLOWERING DOGWOOD

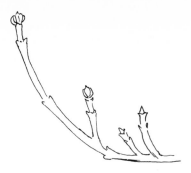

HAWTHORN

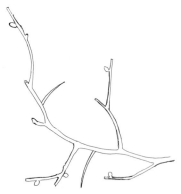

TEA CRAB

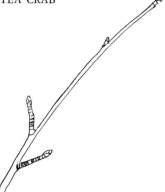

SARGENT CRAB

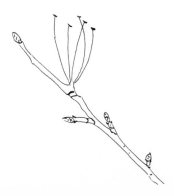

Beautiful turnip-shaped flower buds are held up on the tips of the Dogwood twigs. The leaf buds are cone-shaped. The twigs are purple with a frosty, white bloom.

The slender twigs of the Hawthorn zigzag in every direction, and many are armed with sharp thorns. The dark buds are almost round. The color of the twigs is gray.

Short spurs crowd the branches of this Crabapple, which are scarred by the fallen leaves. The twigs at the ends of the branches are more whiplike. They are dark red-brown. The buds are pinkish, with several scales.

The smooth, reddish twigs of the Sargent Crab have small, pointed buds with greenish, fuzzy scales and pale breathing pores. Many times the stems of the fruit clusters stay on the ends of the spur twigs during the winter.

FRANKLIN TREE
Franklinia alatamaha
size: 18–30 ft.

FRANKLIN TREE
Franklinia alatamaha

This rare, native tree was discovered in 1765 in Georgia by William Bartram, who brought cuttings of it to Philadelphia, where he planted them in his botanical garden. Only the one tree was ever found, and all the Franklin Trees extant today have come from Bartram's original.

The Franklin Tree is a very beautiful, small tree or large shrub. It may grow 18 to 30 feet high. Several ascending branches start from a short trunk and form a rounded, pyramidal head. The twigs are straight, and the winter silhouette has a clean, elegant look. The bark is especially distinctive in winter—smooth, gray with brown stripes. This striped appearance adds interest to any planting when the leaves are gone.

Use the Franklin Tree where it can be featured and enjoyed for its year-round beauty and its late-summer and fall white flowers. Give it room to develop its low branches and show the growing pattern of all the branches without interference.

This tree is hardy as far north as Boston in sheltered places, but it may freeze back and come up from the roots as a shrub that far north. A slightly acid soil and full sun are the best growing conditions for it, although it will stand city conditions. This tree is slow to recover from the shock of transplanting, but once started it is free from pests and diseases.

PYRAMIDAL HORNBEAM
Carpinus betulus var.
pyramidalis
size: 15–20 ft.

PYRAMIDAL HORNBEAM
Carpinus betulus var.
pyramidalis

This is a variety of the European Hornbeam, *Carpinus betulus,* and it is cultivated for its very formal pyramidal shape. The outline is smooth and not wavy, as is the outline of the Lombardy Poplar. The appearance of the whole tree in winter, with its smooth bark, fine twigs, and shapely buds, is elegant.

Long branches start at the base of trunk and flow upwards to make a dense columnar form. This tree grows about 20 feet high at most. Hornbeam is often called Musclewood, because the smooth, grayish blue bark has ridges underneath that look like muscles. It is also called Blue Beech, because of the color of the bark. In winter the slim, pointed, reddish brown buds make a pleasing contrast to the bluish color of the twigs. Often brown leaves hang on for part of the winter.

For formal planting where a sentinel or accent is needed, this Hornbeam is a perfect choice. It will stand shearing to make it more formal, and it will make a very dense hedge. The dynamic shape is a striking contrast to the rounded crowns of other trees. The winter silhouette is strong enough to make a sculptural form.

The Hornbeam likes the moist, deep soil of the river bottoms, but it will adapt well to ordinary growing conditions under cultivation. It is hardy over the eastern half of the United States, excepting Florida and the Gulf coast.

CRAPE MYRTLE
Lagerstroemia indica
size: 10–20 ft.

CRAPE MYRTLE
Lagerstroemia indica

The Crape Myrtle was introduced into this country from China and several tropical countries in 1742. It has become one of the best and most popular flowering trees in the South. As far north as Maryland and Missouri it may be only a shrub, freezing back to the roots in cold winters. Further south, it grows into a large, shrublike tree with multiple trunks or a tree with a single trunk sometimes 20 feet tall.

Crape Myrtle has an unusual, antique look in winter due to the shredded bark that peels off much as does the bark of the Sycamore tree. It has an irregular rounded form. Some of the seedpods and the stalks on which they grew remain at the tips of the branches most of the winter. The branches grow in haphazard fashion and are dense enough in winter to make a good screen.

Like all trees with multiple trunks, Crape Myrtle is useful in landscaping where pattern is needed to soften a building wall or tie down the corner. It makes a good hedge and is beautiful in masses. Since the late-summer flowers bloom on current growth which elongates after the flowering season starts, it can be heavily pruned in winter without spoiling the flowers.

FRANKLIN TREE

PYRAMIDAL HORNBEAM

CRAPE MYRTLE

The straight, slender twigs of the Franklin Tree are brown with a darker brown stripe. The light-colored buds are inconspicuous. The silvery green end bud is fuzzy.

The Hornbeam twigs are a smooth, lustrous iron-gray, with slender, reddish tan, pointed buds. The buds have eight to ten scales. The scars left by the fallen leaves are quite small.

The warm, tan-colored twigs of the Crape Myrtle have a shreddy bark. The buds are small and inconspicuous. In winter, the delicate stems of the dead seed clusters stay on the tips of the twigs for awhile.

Evergreens

Evergreens play a prominent part in the winter scene. At a time when the surrounding landscape is drab and bare, the rich, green foliage and stately contours of the evergreens stand out with compelling interest. The softly waving boughs give protection from winter winds and cover for the birds. The density of the needles makes a perfect background for any beautiful object, the bark of a Paper Birch, a pale-gray Lilac, or a statue.

Evergreens are dignified trees. From a distance most evergreens have pyramidal shapes, at least when they are young, but the texture of the foliage is outstanding enough to identify the tree. Spruce trees appear stiff and spiky. Seven varieties of Spruce grow in our forests. Two outstanding varieties are shown here that are used often in landscaping. The foliage of Pine is softer, with shiny, longer needles in tufts. There are nineteen varieties of pine growing in the United States. Hemlock is very soft and graceful, while Juniper has a dull, muted outline. The flat, shiny sprays of Arbor Vitae are feathery.

It takes special care to use these beautiful trees in landscaping. One should always look ahead with trees, visualizing the amount of space they will need when full grown and their eventual shape, because they change as they grow. This is particularly important with evergreens, since most of them are rapid growers once they are established. In the nursery, they appear as well-behaved, little pyramidal trees that would seem to be perfect for foundation planting or any place in the garden that needs an accent. They are not shrubs and should never be used as planting around the base of the average house. The evergreens need plenty of room to spread at the base and sun and air around them. Some eventually lose their lower branches, which changes the whole aspect of the tree.

Most evergreens are so symmetrical that they stand out sharply in any planting. It is best to use only one or two as individual specimens in an average garden. Use others in groups, masses, or as a screen. The soft, irregular outlines of Hemlock or Juniper are easy to harmonize, while the stiff, pointed tops of Spruce are more dramatic. In parts of the country where Spruce grows naturally, it will look at home in any garden. Elsewhere it may seem more artificial unless the effect is carefully planned. The same is true of Arbor Vitae and Juniper, which look so at home on the rocky hillsides of New England and in the gardens around the houses of that region.

All evergreens of any size above a seedling should be transplanted with a ball of earth.

EASTERN RED CEDAR
Juniperus virginiana

The Eastern Red Cedar is the most widely distributed of the eleven native species of cedar. Over the rocky hillsides of New England and the dry, gravelly banks of the Middle West and South, its slender, evergreen column is a welcome sight in winter In the north, this Juniper grows slowly and remains relatively small. In the richer alluvial soil of the South it may reach a height of 20 to 50 feet. When the tree is young, the branches start at the base, slanting upward to create a pyramidal shape. An older tree may have a bare trunk for several feet and a broader, more open head.

In winter, blue berries with a white bloom grow in sprays among the dark green foliage. Sometimes they are so thick the whole tree looks blue. The birds enjoy them.

Juniper bark is thin and reddish and shreds easily. The trunks of the trees look grooved. This cedar is often mistakenly used in foundation planting. Except in the north, this doesn't work well, since it will grow much too large for the average house. Junipers bought at nurseries have been clipped yearly to make them dense and give them the formal, columnar shape that is so striking in the landscape. Use Junipers as a background for an ornamental feature such as a fountain or a statue. In the winter, the dark green makes a solid background or screen. The spires of dark evergreen add needed variety in shape and texture to the bare deciduous trees. Do not plant Junipers near Apple or Hawthorn, which are hosts to the Cedar rust, a disease that makes unsightly orange galls on the Junipers in the spring and orange spots on the leaves of the Apples and Hawthorns.

Some of the varieties used in landscaping are *Juniperus glauca* with silvery blue foliage, *Juniperus pyramidalis,* and *Juniperus burki.*

CANAERT JUNIPER
Juniperus virginiana var. *canaerti*
size: 20–40 ft.

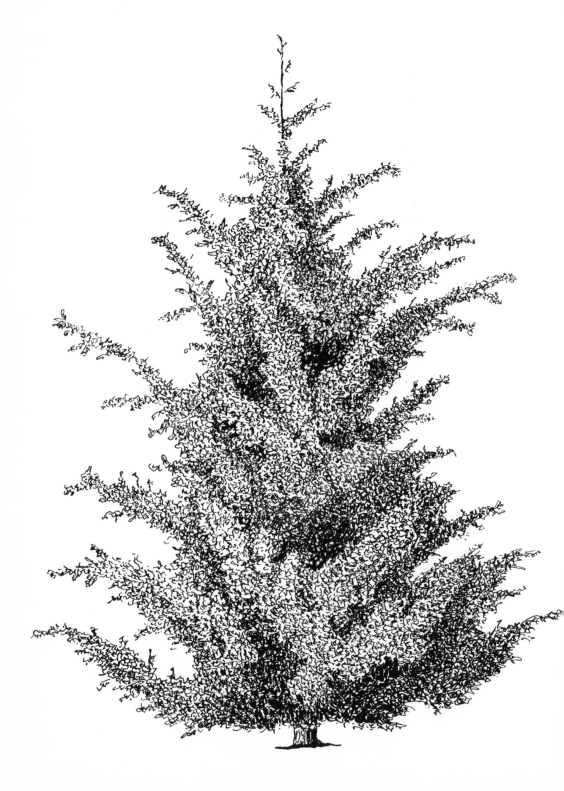

CANAERT JUNIPER
Juniperus virginiana var.
canaerti

This variety of Juniper has been very popular for home planting. In the nursery as a small tree 5 to 6 feet tall, it is seen clipped into a dense pyramidal form, but, if it is not clipped regularly, it soon sends out irregular, spreading branches. It should be grown for its picturesque habit of growth and allowed to develop naturally. Put it where its silhouette will show up. There are plenty of other varieties of Juniper that remain pyramidal and do not need so much pruning.

Canaert Juniper grows in the same habitat as Eastern Red Cedar.

Arbor Vitae or Northern White Cedar is a native of the northern United States. It grows normally in swampy or damp places around the Great Lakes and southward along the Appalachians. It is a pyramidal tree with a dense bushy habit of growth. In the northern part of its range, it often becomes a large tree, sometimes as tall as 50 feet, while as far south as North Carolina, it is a mere shrub. This is just the opposite of the Eastern Red Cedar (*Juniperus virginiana*), which is small in the North and tall in the South. Arbor Vitae is different from most other evergreens also, because it keeps its branches down to the ground until it is an old tree, and it is fairly slow growing.

Often the trunk splits into two or three parts. Sometimes it is twisted, and the orange-brown bark seems to spiral around the trunk. The bark has narrow, deep fissures with interlacing ridges. The fruit is a small cone with six to twelve brown scales that have winged seeds in between. The empty cones stay on the tree all winter.

The foliage of the Arbor Vitae is flat and flexible in lacy sprays. It gives the tree a light, feathery appearance. The Indians called it feather leaf. The bright yellow-green color adds a cheerful note to the darker greens of the other evergreens in winter.

Arbor Vitae stands shearing well, and, because the branches at the base stay bushy, it makes a good hedge. There is a columnar variety (*Thuya occidentalis* var. *pyramidalis*) which is narrower and especially useful for hedges. This is a neat evergreen and a good, dependable tree to use in any formal planting where a columnar accent would be striking. It is also at home in a natural, informal planting.

184

The White Pine is the largest pine in the United States. Its sturdy, gradually tapering trunk was once found as tall as 250 feet or more in the virgin forests where it grew. From Canada south to the Ohio River and down the Alleghenies to northern Georgia it grows well.

It is easy to distinguish the White Pine from other pines by the fineness of the needles, with their blue-green color and also by the horizontal branches on mature trees. The needles grow in clusters of five.

The bark on the young pines is smooth, thin, and greenish brown. As the tree becomes older, the bark becomes dark gray with thick, heavy ridges that are longitudinal and flat topped. The slender pine cones are small and green the first year. During the second summer, they grow longer and turn down from the weight. They can grow 5 to 11 inches long before they mature and turn brown late in the summer.

This pine is good as a specimen on an open lawn or planted as a mass. Because it eventually loses its lower branches, it does not make a good low screen. Use it as a tall screen with other planting in front. Sometimes it will have a double trunk. There is also a columnar variety, *Pinus strobus* var. *fastigiata,* which is excellent for planting where a vertical accent is needed. Remove the leader or terminal, and the tapering top flattens out and becomes picturesque. This shape would be fine to frame a vista or in a Japanese type of landscape.

White Pines are easy to transplant when they are young, as they have a taproot which later on spreads out into a shallow, lateral root system. They like sunshine and will tolerate any soil but a wet one. Never plant White Pine near currant or gooseberry bushes, which are intermediate hosts for the blister rust.

AUSTRIAN PINE
Pinus nigra
size: 45–90 ft.

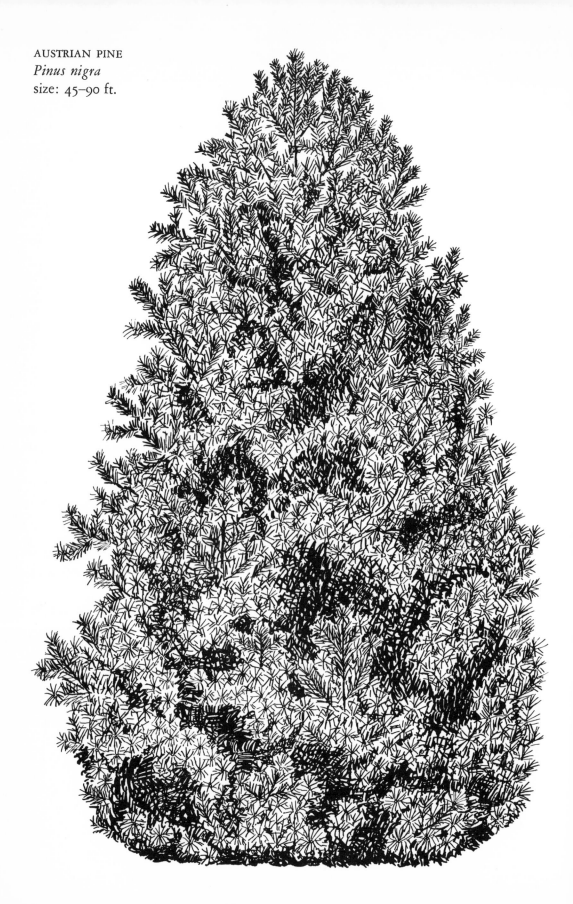

AUSTRIAN PINE
Pinus nigra

The Austrian Pine was one of the earliest evergreens to be imported from Europe. It grows into a large tree with a compact uniform outline that is more symmetrical than other pines. This tree is hardy, fairly fast growing, and will stand dry weather and do well under varying planting conditions.

The stout, brittle branches are yellow-brown when the tree is young but become darker and rougher from the persistent bases of the needle clusters. On old trees, the bark is dark gray-brown, sometimes almost black, with coarse, deep fissures and irregular, scaly ridges.

The color of the foliage is a somber, rich, dark green and the texture is coarse. The 2- to 3-inch cones have no stalk and stand almost at right angles to the branch. They are shiny yellow with thick tips ending in a blunt spine.

Austrian Pines are good for large-scale plantings around public buildings or in parks or cemeteries. In the open, where there is room to develop, the spread of the branches sometimes equals the height of the tree.

TWIG DETAILS

EASTERN RED CEDAR

CANAERT JUNIPER

ARBOR VITAE

WHITE PINE

AUSTRIAN PINE

Red Cedar has two kinds of leaves or needles. The most numerous ones are small, scale-like, blunt-tipped leaves closely pressed to the twigs. On younger trees or at the tips of the more vigorous branches, there are sharp-pointed longer needles, dark green in color.

Since this is a horticultural variety of Eastern Red Cedar, the twigs are similar. Along the reddish stems are small twigs with closely pressed, scale-like, blunt leaves or needles. They are dark green in the fall, turning rusty toward spring. There are blue berries.

Tiny yellow-green leaves cover the twigs and branches in blunt, overlapping scales, so that the twigs themselves look like leaves. The twigs grow in fanlike sprays.

The twigs of the White Pine have soft, flexible, shiny needles in bunches of five. The needles are fine-textured and bluish green, 3 to 5 inches long.

Along the stout twigs of the Austrian Pine there are clusters of needles arranged in bundles of two. The coarse, dark-green needles are stiff, and are about 3 to 5 inches long.

BLUE SPRUCE
Picea pungens
size: 50–70 ft.

BLUE SPRUCE
Picea pungens

The Blue Spruce is one of the most widely admired of all American evergreens. It was originally found in the central Rocky Mountain region, and, although it does best in a cool northern climate, it may be planted as far south as Missouri and the highlands of Georgia.

The shape of the Blue Spruce is symmetrically formal and pyramidal, with branches in layers. The cool, silvery blue color of the crisp foliage is a striking feature. In its native range, it grows fairly rapidly and eventually will reach 70 feet or more. When the tree is over thirty-five years old, the crown becomes more irregular and loses its formal lines. The lower branches die off, so that the trunk shows for about a fourth of its height.

The light, ash-brown bark is made up of many very thin scales that are divided into vertical ridges. The stout twigs are smooth.

The pale, reddish brown cones appear at the top of the tree on the second year twigs. They are about 3 inches long and mature in one season.

This evergreen is best known as an ornamental. Koster's Blue Spruce, *Picea pungens kosteriana,* is the one most sought after for the particularly good blue color of the needles. It is a wonderful tree to use for large-scale formal planting or as a specimen on a lawn, perhaps for a Christmas tree. For a large building, one in the planting on either side of the entrance would be handsome. They do very well near salt water and make a fine windbreak.

NORWAY SPRUCE
Picea excelsa
size: 30–60 ft.

The Norway Spruce, which grows throughout most of Europe, has been widely planted in the United States. Like other Spruces, it prefers a cool climate but will grow as far south as Arkansas and Georgia. It will tolerate any soil but a wet one. In the United States, the Norway Spruce rarely grows over 60 feet tall. Young trees grown in the open have a formal, pyramidal shape. The branches grow in annual whorls or spokes. As the tree becomes large, many small, slender blanchlets hang from the main branches giving the tree a rather mournful appearance, especially since the color of the needles is a somber, dark green.

Norway Spruce is also distinguished from the native varieties by its large cylindrical cones 4 to 7 inches long. They are light brown and hang down when they mature at the end of the first season. The bark is rough with reddish brown scales.

This Spruce keeps its branches down to the ground and is therefore excellent as a background tree or a windbreak. One alone on a lawn is a handsome sight. Groups of Norway Spruce in parks or other large plantings are dignified.

EASTERN HEMLOCK
Tsuga canadensis
size: 45–90 ft.

EASTERN HEMLOCK
Tsuga canadensis

The Eastern Hemlock is one of the most beautiful of our cone-bearing trees. It is more graceful than most evergreens, with its fine twigs and slender, drooping leader at the top. The Hemlock has a dense, conical crown that becomes somewhat irregular as the tree grows old. The trunk is tapering, with deeply divided, cinnamon-red bark with fine scales. The bark eventually becomes 2 to 3 inches thick.

The Hemlock is easily distinguished by the delicate foliage and tiny, perfect cones that hang on the branches. The needles are dark green above and light green underneath, which gives the foliage a silvery look. The Carolina Hemlock (*Tsuga caroliniana*) is especially graceful, with slightly longer needles.

Hemlock ranks high as an ornamental plant. It is slower growing and longer lived than other native conifers. It may live six hundred years. It will stand shearing and makes a good hedge. The fine texture of the needles gives it an elegant appearance that is in keeping with a dignified planting. It is also lovely planted in groups in a natural setting, interspersed with flowering Dogwood or Birch. It will stand shade.

Hemlocks are cool-climate trees. They grow naturally in the northeastern states west to Minnesota and through northern Michigan and Wisconsin, but they are also found along the Appalachian Mountains as far south as Georgia.

TWIG DETAILS   BLUE SPRUCE

NORWAY SPRUCE

EASTERN HEMLOCK

The one half to one inch long needles on the spruce twigs are four sided with sharp points. They cover the twigs on all sides, curving upwards. The color varies from a dull gray-green to a blue-green. At midsummer, the new growth has a silvery white appearance, because of a powdery substance on the surface.

This spruce has shiny, dark-green, pointed needles from one half to one inch long. The needles are attached to the twigs singly on all sides making a thick brush.

Hemlock twigs are slender, with flat, narrow needles about one third to two thirds of an inch long on either side. The ends of the needles are rounded. They are dark green above and light green underneath.

Bibliography

COLLINGWOOD, G. H., *Knowing Your Trees*. Washington, D.C., American Forestry Association, 1937.

EMERSON, ARTHUR I., and WEED, CLARENCE M., D.SC., *Our Trees, How to Know Them,* 5th ed. Garden City, New York, Garden City Publishing Company, 1946.

GRIMM, WILLIAM T., *The Book of Trees.* Harrisburg, Pa., The Stackpole Company, 1957.

JENKINS, CHARLES F., "The Franklin Tree." *Plants and Gardens,* Vol. 6, No. 1 (Spring 1960), p. 56.

LEVISON, J. J., M. F., *The Home Book of Trees and Shrubs,* 2d ed. rev. New York, Alfred A. Knopf, 1949.

MCMINN, HOWARD E., and MAINO, EVELYN, *An Illustrated Manual of Pacific Coast Trees.* Berkeley, University of California Press, 1956.

PETRIDES, GEORGE A., *A Field Guide to Trees and Shrubs.* Boston, Houghton Mifflin Company, 1958.

PHILLIPS, NEILL, "Creating Topiary Pieces." *Trained and Sculptured Plants, A Handbook,* special printing of *Plants and Gardens,* Vol. 17, No. 2, p. 43.

SARGENT, CHARLES SPRAGUE, *Manual of the Trees of North America* (exclusive of Mexico), 2d ed. rev., 2 vol. New York, Dover Publications, Inc., 1965.

SETTERGREN, CARL, and MCDERMOTT, R. E., *Trees of Missouri.* University of Missouri Agricultural Experiment Station, 1962.

WHITNEY, MRS. W. BEAUMONT, "Espaliered Shrubs and Trees." *Trained and Sculptured Plants, A Handbook,* special printing of *Plants and Gardens,* Vol. 17, No. 2, p. 27.

WYMAN, DONALD, "The Best of the Crab Apples." *Plants and Gardens,* Vol. 6, No. 1 (Spring 1960).

Index

ALICE UPHAM SMITH is a well-known landscape architect who is especially qualified to write on gardening subjects. Her formal education included six years in various schools and universities, notably the Cambridge School of Domestic Architecture and Landscape Architecture (now part of Harvard University) and the University of Edinburgh in Scotland. She has taught landscape gardening privately, in adult extension classes, and at the University of Missouri, where she resided until her husband's retirement in 1966. In addition to a large private practice in Columbia, Missouri, she was the landscape consultant at Stephens College for many years. A writer and lecturer, Mrs. Smith now lives in Mountain Home, Arkansas. She is a regular contributor to the Garden Section of *The New York Times,* and her articles have appeared in *Popular Gardening, Flower and Garden,* and *Woman's Day.* She is also the author of *Patios, Terraces, Decks, and Roof Gardens* (1969).